Lab Manual to Accompany
The Complete Guide to Servers and Server+

Michael Graves

THOMSON

DELMAR LEARNING

Australia   Canada   Mexico   Singapore   Spain   United Kingdom   United States

THOMSON

DELMAR LEARNING

Lab Manual to Accompany The Complete Guide to Servers and Server+

Michael Graves

Vice President, Technology and Trades Academic Business Unit:
David Garza

Director of Learning Solutions:
Sandy Clark

Acquisitions Editor:
Nick Lombardi

Senior Product Manager:
Michelle Ruelos Cannistraci

Marketing Director:
Deborah S. Yarnell

Marketing Manager:
Guy Baskaran

Marketing Coordinator:
Shanna Gibbs

Director of Production:
Patty Stephan

Production Manager:
Andrew Crouth

Editorial Assistant:
Dawn Daugherty

ISBN-13: 978-1-4180-2024-8
ISBN-10: 1-4180-2024-9

NOTICE TO THE READER

BRIEF
Contents

TABLE OF
Contents

Introduction

Welcome to the Lab Manual for *The Complete Guide to Servers and Server+*. The labs included in this manual have been specifically designed to provide the student with some hands-on experience in the installation, configuration, and troubleshooting of operating systems. Still, there is going to be a bit of exposure to the system hardware as well. So it wouldn't hurt to have a basic understanding in that area of expertise.

In order to accomplish the exercises in these labs the classrooms will have to be equipped with some basic necessities. These include a PC for each of the students with the following minimum specifications.

- 700Mhz CPU
- 256MB RAM
- 20GB hard disk drive
- Floppy diskette drive
- CD-ROM drive
- Keyboard
- Mouse
- SVGA monitor
- One available PCI slot
- A copy of Windows 2000 Server (not yet installed)

In addition, the students will need the following:

- A SCSI host adapter
- A SCSI cable
- Two SCSI hard disks
- Two IDE hard disks
- A SCSI tape drive
- A SCSI cable
- Access to the Internet

These labs are going to provide students an opportunity to get their hands a bit dirty as they encounter a large number of the CompTIA objectives for the Server+ Exam. Unfortunately, since the exam is theoretical as well as practical, there are objectives that won't be covered. For those, you'll need to rely on your textbook. In addition, since the textbook and lab manual are designed to be more inclusive than simply passing the Server+ exam, there are exercises that are related to server management that do not map to any CompTIA objective. In each lab, the objectives covered are listed at the beginning.

You will notice as you go through the labs that the same objectives will appear in different labs, again and again. This shouldn't come as much of a surprise since each of these objectives includes a number of subcomponents. So don't get tied up in the details to the point that you don't have fun and *learn!*

1

BUILDING A NETWORK SERVER

<table>
<tr><td colspan="2">CompTIA Server+ Objectives Covered in This Lab</td></tr>
<tr><td>1.1</td><td>Know the characteristics, purpose, function, limitations, and performance of the system bus architectures.</td></tr>
<tr><td>1.4</td><td>Know the function of the application server models.</td></tr>
<tr><td>1.5</td><td>Know the characteristics of the following types of memory and server memory requirements.</td></tr>
<tr><td>1.6</td><td>Know differences between different SCSI solutions, their advantages, and their specifications.</td></tr>
<tr><td>1.11</td><td>Know the characteristics of hot swap drives and hot plug boards.</td></tr>
<tr><td>1.12</td><td>Know the features, advantages, and disadvantages of multiprocessing.</td></tr>
<tr><td>1.14</td><td>Understand the processor subsystem of a server.</td></tr>
</table>

A vast number of computer hardware technicians do this. Look on the front bezel of their own personal computer to see what brand they prefer. And what brand do you find as often as not? No brand at all. Rather than trust a system put together from parts supplied by the lowest bidder, many technicians choose to purchase the parts they need from reliable vendors and assemble their own computers. This allows the technician to choose each component that goes into the system based on his or her own set of priorities.

The priorities are established based on a simple question. What is the primary use for this system? I discussed this in detail throughout the textbook. Different applications have different requirements. For the person who needs nothing more complicated than an intelligent type-writer (Mom, what's a typewriter?), then there isn't much need for a system with huge amounts of horsepower. On the other hand, the avid gamer or the digital photographer has discovered that the more computer horsepower the system has, the easier their work is. Well, the faster it is, at least.

This lab focuses on building a network server. I strongly recommend that this lab be introduced early in the semester so that the students can be thinking about their configurations as they are introduced to the various components and their functions as the course progresses.

BUILDING THE NETWORK SERVER

In this exercise, I'm going to have you build (on paper, anyway) a network server designed to run Windows 2003 Advanced Server. It will service a network of 500 users and must accommodate Microsoft Exchange Server, an Oracle database and store the user files for all those users. In order to complete this exercise, there are a few things you will need to know. For this information, refer to *The Complete Guide to Servers and Server+* textbook.

This is an exercise in theory, rather than reality. So the only materials you will need are a good imagination, a pencil, and paper (a word processor will do if that's all you can come up with) and a viable Internet connection. The students are not expected to actually purchase the parts and build the system. However, should you choose to do so and would like to have your system evaluated, send me an e-mail and I'll provide you with a shipping address. I'll be happy to put your finished product through its paces for a year or so and then I'll get it right back to you.

The dream system that you're aspiring to create must be capable of several different, and in many cases, complex tasks. It must be able to handle all those simultaneous logins in the morning when everyone arrives for work. It must not only store the database, but it must secure it and keep it safe from file corruption. Most of all, it must be reliable.

Performance Considerations

Now, I'll be the first to admit that a large number of off-the-shelf computer systems sold by the vast majority of major manufacturers are capable of running all of the above applications. The key to this assignment is that you are designing your own system as a way of getting around the performance compromises inherent in any of the prefabricated machines. The type of server generally dictates overall requirements. In Chapter 1 of the textbook, I discussed different types of servers and their requirements. Review that material and consider the requirements of the one you are designing.

Processing

A couple of the applications in your list are extremely processor intensive. Therefore, you need to design your system so that the processor does not become a bottleneck. Refer to Chapter 6 for a more detailed discussion of different processor features to consider. Also consider the impact of SMP on your server and make an informed decision as to whether this system justifies adding the feature.

Memory

Nearly all of the listed applications are hungry for as much memory as you can throw at them. However, this is definitely an area where sheer quantity will not be your only ally. You must not only design your system with sufficient memory for the task at hand, but the appropriate type of memory. Review Chapter 7 before committing to a decision. What services are going to be running in addition to the applications?

I/O Bus

Most of the applications you will be running will be moving huge quantities of data back and forth across the different system busses. The various components you choose for your system will need to attach to these busses. It won't matter much if you've picked the perfect CPU/Memory combination if you're trying to move all that data over an 8.33MHz ISA network card. But you won't be trying that. Will you? Perhaps a second reading of Chapter 8 will help.

Graphics

Graphics is an area in which the gamers among you might have to think a little bit outside the box. Sure, you are already up to date on all the fastest gaming cards and what makes them tick. But is speed the issue here? Your audience is one or two geeks who only visit the machine when there's a problem. Usually. Pretend that you don't see that copy of Renegade Alien Rednecks installed.

Hard Disk Storage

These days, the size of your disk isn't what matters, but how you use it. The smallest hard disk manufactured today will provide sufficient space for all of your applications and still leave room for several projects like the one described in this exercise. The challenge here is to store it all, protect it all, and make sure that 500 users don't all start complaining at once about how slow the server is.

Alternative Storage

There are many options for alternative storage. Research the available options and decide which is best for your purposes.

The Enclosure

Now we need to find a home of all these fancy new components. It probably won't be such a great idea to simply spread them out over the counter and run wires and cables back and forth between them. Also, what about all those drives we've selected? What do we do with them? We need a computer case. But what kind of case do we need, and just where are we going to put it?

Ulterior Considerations

Now here's the real kicker. In reality, you aren't the network administrator in our little scenario. You are a sales representative for a company that specializes in custom configurations and you're designing this machine for a client. These are the performance demands you must meet, but you're in competition with several other companies. These companies are your other classmates. For this project, there will be only one A. And that will be the computer that most successfully meets the performance demands, but at the lowest price. Your instructor is the purchasing agent that you must please and his or her final judgment is all that matters.

2

RUNNING DIAGNOSTICS

The following CompTIA exam objectives will be covered in these lab exercises:

2.1 Identify common symptoms and problems associated with each module and how to troubleshoot and isolate the problems.

Troubleshooting is both a science and an art. When it comes to the art, you either have it or you don't. Many people are able to develop it over time with practice. The science, on the other hand, is something one can learn. The first half of this lab will lead you through some of the diagnostic procedures utilizing some of the freeware diagnostics utilities that are available. The second section of this lab is optional, depending on whether your class is able to provide a POST Card for the procedures. To finish both of these labs, you will need:

- The Student machine for each student, booted to Windows

- A blank, formatted floppy 3.5" 1.44MB floppy diskette

- Tuff Test Lite (latest version; Lab was written with v. 1.53)

- For the optional lab, the classroom will need at least one POST Card hardware diagnostics tool. Any brand will do. This lab was written using the Ultra-X PCI POST Card

- A pencil and paper

Exercise 1: Software Diagnostics

This exercise will examine Tuff Test Lite. Although it may not be the most potent piece of diagnostic software available, it has the advantage of being free and performs the diagnostics that I want to demonstrate in this lab. Should you choose to purchase the Professional version later, some of the glaring limitations of the free version are eliminated, making the program a potent contender.

1. Start by downloading and installing Tuff Test Lite onto your PC. When prompted, insert your blank, formatted diskette into the drive and make the bootable floppy as prompted by the installation routine. This cannot simply be added to your Technician's Boot Diskette because the tests must be run independently of any OS. Your TBD loads a basic Windows kernel. As such, devices dependent on Windows drivers might not be tested.

2. Once the bootable floppy has been completed, restart your machine with the floppy still inserted in the drive. There will be two introductory screens, one introducing the product and another promoting the Single-user and Professional versions of its more sophisticated products. Next is the main menu. You have precisely 10 seconds to decide what you want to do on this screen or it will automatically assume that you wish to run every test available. We don't want to run all the tests, so press F2. A screen similar to the one seen in **Figure L2-1** should appear.

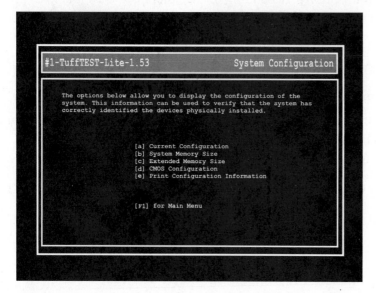

Figure L2-1   The View Configuration Page of Tuff Test Lite

3. Note that the options are to view:
   a. Current Configuration
   b. System Memory Size
   c. Extended Memory Size
   d. CMOS Configuration
   e. Print Configuration information
   f. Press F1 to return to the main menu

4. After viewing each of the above options, press F1 to return to the main menu. Now we have more time to explore this menu (**Figure L2-2**).

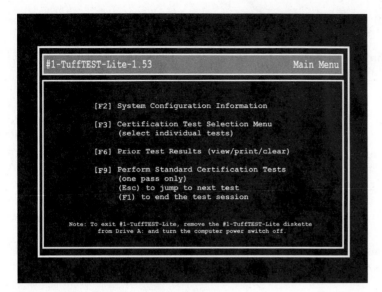

```
#1-TuffTEST-Lite-1.53                              Main Menu

        [F2] System Configuration Information

        [F3] Certification Test Selection Menu
             (select individual tests)

        [F6] Prior Test Results (view/print/clear)

        [F9] Perform Standard Certification Tests
             (one pass only)
             (Esc) to jump to next test
             (F1)  to end the test session

        Note: To exit #1-TuffTEST-Lite, remove the #1-TuffTEST-Lite diskette
              from Drive A: and turn the computer power switch off.
```

Figure L2-2   Tuff Test Main Menu

5. The first option, F2, simply brings you back to the configuration menu that you just examined. F3 allows you to select the different tests that you wish to perform. These options include:

   a. System Board Tests
       i. Microprocessor
       ii. Math Coprocessor
       iii. DMA Controller
       iv. Real Time Clock
   b. Video Alignment Aids
       i. Cross-hatch Pat(tern)
       ii. Dot Pattern
       iii. Vertical Bars
       iv. Horizontal Bars
       v. Text Color Chart
   c. Video Adapter Tests
       i. Verify Screen Mem(ory)
       ii. Character Set
       iii. Video Attributes
       iv. Fill Display
       v. Cursor Addressing
       vi. Video Memory
       vii. High-Res Color
       viii. Text Resolution
   d. Parallel Port Tests
       i. LPT1 (I/O Address)
       ii. LPT2 (I/O Address)
       iii. LPT3 (I/O Address)
   e. Serial Port Tests
       i. COM1 (I/O Address)
       ii. COM2 (I/O Address)
       iii. COM3 (I/O Address)
       iv. COM4 (I/O Address)

f. Diskette Drive (A:) Tests
  i. Reset Drive
  ii. Rotational Timing
  iii. Seek/Read
  iv. Read Only
g. Diskette Drive (B:) Tests
  i. Reset Drive
  ii. Rotational Timing
  iii. Seek/Read
  iv. Read Only
h. Fixed Disk (0) Tests
  i. Controller
  ii. Seek (Hysteresis)
  iii. Surface Test
i. Fixed Disk (0) Tests
  i. Controller
  ii. Seek (Hysteresis)
  iii. Surface Test
j. Main Memory Tests
  i. All Zeros
  ii. All Ones
  iii. Checkerboard
  iv. Address
  v. Walking Ones
k. Extended Memory Tests
  i. All Zeros
  ii. All Ones
  iii. Checkerboard
  iv. Address
  v. Walking Ones

6. You can toggle individual tests on or off by typing the number specific to that test, as viewed on the screen. Entire groupings of tests are toggled on or off by typing the letter for that test. In order to run all tests from this menu, press F8 and let the tests run. As they do so, read the following text explaining these tests.

- CPU: In this particular program, the manufacturer does not specify what tests are being performed. I was, however, able to determine that at the minimum a test for the accuracy of speed is performed.

- Math Coprocessor: Tests the MathCo section for floating-point errors.

- DMA Controller: Queries and checks responses to each DMA channel in the system.

- Real Time Clock: Queries and checks responses to RCT and alarm functions.

- Crosshatch Pattern: Tests the monitor's ability to display images created by multiple crossing lines.

- Dot Pattern: Tests the monitor's ability to display images created by a montage of multi-colored dots.

- Vertical Bars: Draws patterns created primarily by bars running up and down the screen.

- Horizontal Bars: Draws patterns created primarily by bars running across the screen.

2

- Text Color Chart: Displays the different colors in which text can be displayed.

- Verify Screen Mem(ory): Tests the memory in an address space reserved for the information to be sent to the video card.

- Character Set: Verifies that characters from the standard ACSII character set can be displayed.

- Video Attributes: Tests non-text characteristics of the display, such as brightness, color rendition, flash accuracy, and intensity.

- Fill Display: The entire screen is filled with characters, testing its ability to compose and then properly display these characters. It also tests the screen's ability to autowrap text.

- Cursor Addressing: Translates the addressing sequence that identifies where the screen cursor should appear and confirms that the cursor appears at the correct location.

- Video Memory: Sends multiple sets of data to memory installed on the video adapter and confirms that identical data is provided by that memory when read back.

- Hi-Res Color: Tests color rendition at higher resolutions than standard VGA.

- Text Resolution: Tests the reproduction text at various resolutions.

- Parallel Port (1, 2, and 3): Performs an I/O operation across the parallel ports and reports the I/O address of that port. Requires that a loopback adapter be installed on the port being tested.

- Serial Port (1, 2, 3, and 4): Performs an I/O operation across the serial ports and reports the I/O address of that port. Requires that a loopback adapter be installed on the port being tested.

- Reset Drive: Tests the integrity of the Change Drive signal that informs the controller that the diskette in the drive has been changed.

- Rotational Timing: Confirms that the Read/Write heads are in synch with the rotational speed of the motor.

- Seek/Read: Tests the drive's ability to locate a specific piece of data and read it back to memory.

- Read Only: Performs a read operation from a pre-selected sector and compares the data it finds to that which the test is expecting.

- Controller: Tests the ability of the hard disk's controller to queue and execute commands properly.

- Seek (Hysteresis): Performs a series of I/O operations requiring that the data be located and tracked by the controller.

- Surface Test: Examines each cluster on the drive for damaged or weak sectors.

- All Zeros: Fills all available memory with 0s and then reads it back, looking for the presence of any 1s.

- All Ones: Fills all available memory with 1s and then reads it back, looking for the presence of any 0s.

- Checkerboard: Alternates 0s and 1s across the memory matrix in a checkerboard pattern and then reads it back, looking for any deviations in the pattern.

- Address: Writes data to each available memory address and then performs an I/O operation to that address to verify that the data written is found at the proper address.

- Walking Ones: Takes a pattern consisting of several contiguous 1s, while the remainder of free memory is written to 0s, and moves the block of 1s in increments equaling the number of 1s in that block up through the remainder of available memory. In a system with a large amount of RAM, this test can take quite a long time.

Exercise 1 Review

As you can see, troubleshooting does not have to be trial and error. With the proper tools at your disposal, a lot of the guesswork can be eliminated.

1. Why are you unable to run Tuff Test from your Technician's Boot Diskette?

2. Why is Tuff Test unable to test certain devices, such as modems and sound cards? (Be careful here, you might have to think back to material presented in the textbook to answer this one!)

3. As noted in the lab, in order to test either a serial port or a parallel port using Tuff Test (or most other diagnostics programs, for that matter) a loopback adapter must be installed. Why do you think this is the case?

EXERCISE 2: WORKING WITH A POST CARD (OPTIONAL)

A POST Card (**Figures L2.3** and **L2.4**) is a hardware diagnostics tool that reads BIOS calls throughout the process of POST. You simply insert the card into an available expansion slot (usually PCI, but some of the older ones are ISA), and turn on the computer. An LED display flashes result codes for each POST operation until the boot process fails. At that point, the error number displayed shows what process was active when POST failed and, therefore, what component failed. To perform this exercise, you will need a POST Card and the accompanying diagnostics manual along with a computer that is unable to complete POST. You can create the latter by removing the memory or video card. Note that without the manual you won't be able to interpret the codes.

Figure L2-3   The PCI POST Card does not look like any other expansion card, except for the little LED display in the upper right-hand corner.

1. To come up with an unbootable machine, remove either the memory or the video card.

2. Examine the motherboard to determine the brand and version of BIOS installed.

3. Insert the PCI POST Card into any free expansion slot of the appropriate type.

4. Power up the machine.

5. Record the last code displayed. Depending on the brand, this code may be displayed in either decimal or hexadecimal notation.

6. Look up the code in the manual. It will tell you where the failure occurred.

Figure L2-4   When inserted, it's easy for the LED display to be blocked by other devices.

Exercise 2 Review

1. Why do you suppose knowing the make and version of the BIOS of the machine you're testing is so critical?

2. How can the POST Card tell you what process failed if that process, in reality, failed?

3

A Tour of the BIOS

CompTIA exam objectives covered in this lab include:

1.1 Identify basic terms, concepts, and functions of system modules, including how each module should work during normal operation and during the boot process.

2.1 Identify common symptoms and problems associated with each module and how to troubleshoot and isolate the problems.

4.4 Identify the purpose of CMOS (Complementary Metal-Oxide Semiconductor), what it contains, and how to change its basic parameters.

Considering the system BIOS is responsible for starting the computer, making sure the system devices work properly, and speaking to the CPU on its terms, it's probably a good idea if the average technician knows how to configure it properly. As I discussed in Chapter 5 of the textbook, three executable programs reside on the BIOS. These programs are Power On, Self Test (POST), Setup, and Bootstrap Loader. This lab will describe some of the more common settings of Setup. For more information on POST and Bootstrap Loader, refer to Chapter 5 of the textbook. For this lab, all you need is the Student System equipped with KB and monitor. You won't even need the mouse.

One thing I should point out before you proceed is that I will be using an Award BIOS in the lab. Machines with an AMI BIOS should be very similar, but there will be some differences as to what setting appears. In fact, you may have an Award BIOS and get a somewhat different screen. However, you will see enough of the settings I describe, and their descriptions will be similar enough to make the exercise worthwhile. If the machines you use are equipped with a Phoenix BIOS, another brand not mentioned, or a BIOS generated by a major computer manufacturer, then you will most likely find that following this lab step by step is inconvenient and confusing. Simply go through their various menu options and try to associate the entries you find with the ones in this lab whenever possible.

EXERCISE 1: A TOUR OF THE BIOS

1. First make sure the monitor is on and running before starting the machine. Monitors frequently take longer to get up and running. Next, you must press the key sequence needed to enter the Setup program.

2. Turn on the system and watch carefully. Somewhere on the screen, usually in either the upper right-hand corner or centered near the bottom of the screen, there will be a message telling you what key to press to enter the Setup program. If you are using proprietary machines with a splash screen that appears on startup, you can usually exit the splash screen by pressing the <Esc> key. If your machine give no indication of what keys to press, try some of the following:

   a. <Delete>: Award, AMI and some proprietary.

   b. <F2>: Dell and some Phoenix

   c. <F10>: Compaq and some Phoenix

   d. <Ctrl><Alt><Delete>: Some proprietary

   e. <Esc>Some proprietary

3. Those of you running Award or AMI will be rewarded with a screen that looks like the one in **Figure L3-1**. Depending on the brand of motherboard and how old of a version your BIOS is, the categories may vary from machine to machine.

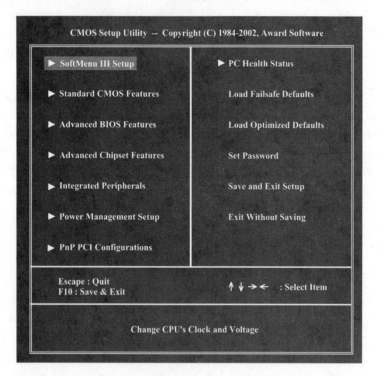

Figure L3-1   The opening screen for an Award BIOS

4. For the remainder of this exercise, we will go through the categories one by one and I will explain the meaning of each setting and the effect it has on your machine, including any ill effects of an incorrect setting. Because so many different people will be seeing so many different screens, I won't be using screenshots for the remainder of this lab because this will confuse those not using Award BIOS.

5. Soft Menu III Setup: This menu option will only appear on motherboards that support BIOS configuration of CPU parameters. There are four main user-configurable parameters.

   a. CPU Operating Speed: There will be sub-parameters listed below that are grayed out because Intel has locked certain parameters, including CPU multiplier. However, the CPU can be set to run beyond or below its rated speed. Changing CPU operating speed will affect some of these parameters. A change that defines a multiplier not supported by the CPU will prevent the system from booting, and in most cases automatically start Setup during the next attempt so that you can fix the problem.

b. DRAM Clock: The options on this particular version are Host Clock and HCLK-PCICLK. The Host Clock is the speed of the front-side bus (FSB). The PCI clock is 33MHz. If the FSB is set at 133MHz in the CPU Operating Speed, then selecting Host Clock means that your DRAM will operate at that same speed. Setting it at HCLK-PCICLK means that RAM will operate at the host clock speed *minus* the PCI clock speed, or 100MHz in this case. This allows you to use memory designed for slower systems on this computer.

c. CPU Power Supply: The options are CPU Default or User Defined. CPU Default auto-detects two settings, Core Voltage and VCC3 voltage. Core Voltage is the voltage that powers the CPU and VCC3 voltage is the voltage that exists between the CPU and I/O. Typically Core can range from around 1.3 to 2.8V. This particular board supports 1.3V to 1.85V. Unless you are attempting to overclock your system, these settings should remain at default settings. However, if you attempt to run your CPU beyond its rated speed, it may be necessary to bump these settings up a notch. Be forewarned that doing so can make your system unstable.

d. CPU Hardwired IRQ: By default PCI devices have four IRQ channels. The options here are 4 and 1. The default is 4 and should remain that way unless someone at the manufacturer's technical support line instructs you to change it. Setting it to 1 will cause the system to check only one channel during POST. If that channel's IRQ is already taken, it will record a conflict and the device won't be recognized. Setting it to 4 forces POST to scan all four channels.

6. Standard CMOS Features: This is where features common to all computer systems are recorded. With a couple of minor possible exceptions, nothing in here will prevent your system from booting if a setting is incorrect.

a. Date: Sets the date

b. Time: Sets the time (well, what did you think?)

c. IDE Primary Master: Auto, User Defined, None. Auto lets the system query the hard disk for its parameters and adjusts the settings accordingly. User Defined allows the user to input the number of cylinders, heads, sectors/track, and a predefined landing zone. None shuts off that particular channel and no device attached to it will be recognized.

d. IDE Primary Slave: See above

e. IDE Secondary Master: See above

f. IDE Secondary Slave: See above

g. Drive A: Your primary floppy drive. Options may include 360KB 5.25", 1.2MB 5.25", 720KB 3.5", 1.44MB 3.5", and possibly 2.88MB 3.5". There will also be an option for None. On some versions of BIOS, None is the default option and the system will revert to None if power is cut off from the CMOS chip for too long. Setting this parameter to None will cause the system to ignore the floppy on bootup, making it inaccessible to the user. Setting it incorrectly will cause errors in POST and if you choose to continue, the floppy drive will not be readable once the system is booted.

h. Drive B: Your secondary floppy drive (if installed). See above.

i. Floppy 3 Mode Support. This is a Japanese standard that stores 1.2MB on a standard 3.5" high-density floppy diskette. If you have a floppy drive that supports this mode and you wish to enable it, the options are None, Drive A, Drive B, and Both.

j. Video: The options are EGA/VGA, CGA40, CGA80, and Mono. I know of no monitor manufacturers still making CGA or the old-style Hercules mono-mode monitors. Unless you managed to stumble across one of these archeological finds and have some masochistic desire to actually *use* it, the default setting of EGA/VGA should not be changed.

k. Halt On: Defines what POST errors can be ignored. Typical settings are None, All But Keyboard, All But Diskette, and All But Disk/Key. Keyboards occasionally exhibit "phantom errors." Even if the keyboard is not found, it may be preferable to let the system boot. Many systems allow a PS2 or a USB keyboard to be inserted on the fly after POST is completed. Some people rarely, if ever use their floppy drive. Having their entire machine become unusable because that drive has failed would be unacceptable.

7. Now I'll move on to the Advanced BIOS Features. Most of the settings are safe enough and cause no more harm than seriously reduced system performance if incorrect. A couple of features that I'll point out can possibly prevent your system from booting. If that happens, restart the machine, enter Setup and restore the system to Factory Defaults. I'll be covering that a little later in this lab.

   a. Virus Warning: Enable or Disable. Prevents the system from making changes to either BIOS code (if the BIOS is flashable) or the hard disk's master boot record. This may need to be disabled when reinstalling an operating system.

   b. Cache Level 1: Enable or Disable. Enables read/write operations to L1 cache built into CPU. Disable *only* if you know you have a CPU such as the original Celeron that has no L1 cache onboard.

   c. Cache Level 2: Enables read/write operations to L2 cache built into CPU. On older motherboards, the L2 may be located on the system board. Disable *only* if you know you have a CPU such as the original Celeron that has no L2 cache onboard.

   d. CPU Level 2 Cache ECC Check: Enabled/Disabled. Turns on/off use of Error Correction Code.

   e. Quick Power On Self Test, Enabled/Disabled, Full Test. Tests only selected system components on cold boot.

   f. HDD Sequence, IDE/SCSI, Where to look for MBR Boot Sequence, Options vary. Determines the order of devices in which POST looks for the MBR.

   g. Boot Up Floppy Seek, Enabled/Disabled. Tests floppy drive to see if it has 40 or 80 tracks.

   h. Floppy Disk Access Control, R/W, Read Only. Security Access for floppy drive.

   i. HDD S.M.A.R.T capability: Enabled/Disabled. If your hard disk supports Self Monitoring And Reporting Technology (and everything made for the past several years does) then this should be enabled. To take advantage of it, you'll need to install a utility on your system as well.

   j. PS2 Mouse Function Control: Enabled/Auto. Looks to PS2 for mouse.

   k. OS2 Onboard Memory: Enabled/Disabled. Use memory mapping functions as defined by IBM's OS2 operating system. Unless you are actually running a copy of that now-defunct OS, this should be disabled.

   l. Video ROM/BIOS Shadowing: Enabled/Disabled. Allows copying of BIOS routines from your video card to upper memory for enhanced performance. Enabled is best unless you are told otherwise by your manufacturer.

   m. C8000-DFFFF Shadowing (multiple entries), Enabled/Disabled. Allows copying of Supplemental BIOS routines of specific devices to specific addresses. Enable *only* if the installation instructions for a specific device instructs you to do so. In that case, the manufacturer will also let you know which address range (or ranges) to use.

   n. Boot Up NumLock Status: On/Off. Determines whether number lock on keyboard is on or off after system boots.

   o. Typomatic Rate Setting: Disabled/Enabled. Disabled turns off Typomatic Rate and Typomatic Delay.

   p. Typomatic Rate, Options vary. Sets speed at which characters repeat when a key on the keyboard is held down.

   q. Typomatic Delay, Options vary. Sets time that elapses before keys begin to repeat when a key on the keyboard is held down.

   r. Security Option, System/Setup. Determines to what any security settings you configure will apply. System dictates that a password will be needed to boot the system. Setup allows the user to boot the system without a password, but requires a password to run the CMOS Setup Utility (the one you're currently examining). Security Settings are found elsewhere in the BIOS.

8. Now we'll enter the possibly intimidating and potentially dangerous arena of the Chipset Features Setup. This is where an incorrect setting can render your system useless until corrected. As with the Advanced BIOS Features, you simply reboot, reset to Factory Defaults, and start over.

    a. EDO Autoconfiguration: Enabled/Disabled. Allows chipset to control timing functions for Extended Data Out (EDO) memory. This and the other EDO-specific functions will not appear on a system that does not support EDO. (That shouldn't be much of a surprise.)

    b. EDO Read Burst Timing: Varies. Sets number of clock cycles for Burst Mode read operations. Setting any of this or the following memory timing parameters too fast can prevent the system from booting. Setting them too slow will theoretically hinder performance.

    c. EDO Write Burst Timing: Varies. Sets number of clock cycles for Burst Mode write operations.

    d. EDO RAS Precharge: 3T, 4T. Sets number of clock cycles for RAS Precharge.

    e. EDO RAS/CAS Delay: 2T, 3T. Sets number of clock cycles for RAS/CAS Delay.

    f. SDRAM Configuration: Varies. Sets clock speed of SDRAM.

    g. SDRAM RAS Precharge: Auto, 3T, 4T. Sets number of clock cycles for RAS Precharge.

    h. SDRAM RAS/CAS Delay: Auto, 3T, 2T. Sets number of clock cycles for RAS/CAS Delay.

    i. Graphics Aperture Size: Varies. Setting it too low can result in degraded video performance, but on the other hand, setting it too high takes memory away from applications running on the system should another application take full advantage of the setting.

    j. PCI 2.1 Support: Enabled/Disabled. Disabled setting drops system back to PCI Version 1.0.

    k. Memory Hole at 15M-16M: Enabled/Disabled. ISA Devices can only read up to 16MB of RAM because of their 24-bit address space. Some very old ISA devices have compatibility issues with extended memory beyond 16MB and the area between 15MB and 16MB needs to be reserved as a buffer "window" for bringing data down from that area. Unless you are using one of these older cards, this should be disabled.

    l. Onboard FDC Controller: Enabled/Disabled. Allows you to disable the floppy disk drive.

    m. Onboard Floppy Swap A/B: Enabled/Disabled. Has no effect of which floppy drive is bootable, but once POST is completed, it switches drives A and B so that the primary drive is listed as B and vice versa.

    n. Onboard Parallel Port: Various settings/Disabled. Allows disabling or reconfiguring the parallel port to a different LPT port.

    o. Parallel Port Mode : Normal, ECC, ECC/ECP. Sets up parallel communications.

    p. ECP DMA Select: Varies. Sets DMA channel used by ECP Parallel mode. Grayed out if a parallel mode other than ECP is configured.

    q. UART2 Use Infrared: Enabled/Disabled. Sets infrared port to UART2.

    r. Onboard PCI/IDE Enable: Both, Primary, Secondary, Disabled. Enables/disables IDE ports.

    s. IDE DMA Mode: Auto/Disable. Disables, autoselects Direct Memory Access mode for IDE devices.

    t. IDE 0/1 Master/Slave: Various. Sets PIO mode and DMA channel for specific device.

    u. CPU/PCI Write Buffer: Enable/Disable. When enabled sets up a memory cache for data being moved from the PCI bus to the CPU. Unless otherwise specified by the manufacturer, this should be enabled.

    v. PCI Dynamic Bursting: Enable/Disable. When enabled, combines multiple 8- or 16-bit write executions into 32-bit operations. Some older PCI NICs are not compatible with this option, but otherwise, this setting should be enabled for best performance. If your NIC is incompatible, it won't work, so this is one area to look when troubleshooting an older PCI NIC you just installed.

9. Integrated Peripherals: Here is where many of the settings for devices such as the IDE ports, floppy ports, and serial ports are set. Systems with embedded peripherals such as onboard sound and video will likely see a number of other settings here as well.

   a. Onboard IDE-1 Controller: Enabled/Disabled. Allows the user to turn the controller off or on as required.

      i. –Master Drive PIO Mode: Modes 0-4. Sets Programmed Input Output mode for the device on this channel.

      ii. –Slave Drive PIO Mode: Same as above.

      iii. –Master Drive DMA Mode: Modes 1–5. Sets Ultra DMA Mode for device on this channel.

      iv. –Slave Drive DMA Mode: Modes 1–5. Same as above.

   b. Onboard IDE-2 Controller. All of the parameters and subsequent parameters for PIO and DMA modes are the same as above.

   c. IDE Prefetch Mode: Enabled/Disabled. On drives that support this function, it allows the controller to initiate the read process for the next sectors of data that are likely to be needed. If a hard disk is constantly generating drive read errors after the boot process is completed, try disabling this setting.

   d. Init Display First: PCI/AGP. If two graphics adapters are installed in the computer, this setting determines which is the primary and which is the secondary adapter.

   e. USB Controller: Enabled/Disable. Turns the Universal Serial Bus controller on/off.

      i. USB Keyboard Support: OS/BIOS. Determines whether a USB keyboard will be managed by the BIOS or the operating system.

   f. HDD Block Mode: Options Vary. Dictates the number of sectors a hard drive can transfer during each interrupt request. With modern drives the maximum setting is reported by the drive during POST and the value should not be set higher than the default. It can prevent the system from booting. A lower setting can resolve buffer overflows.

   g. Onboard FDD Controller: Enabled/Disabled. Turns on/off the floppy disk drive controller as needed.

   h. Onboard Serial Port 1: Various COM port settings/Disabled. Allows disabling or reconfiguring Serial Port 1 to a different COM port.

   i. Onboard Serial Port 2: Various settings/Disabled. Allows disabling or reconfiguring Serial Port 2 to a different COM port.

10. Power Management Setup: These days conserving energy is of concern to everyone. Or at least it should be. A company that lets its computers run 24 hours a day, seven days a week, even when there are only users available eight hours a day, five days a weeks, wastes a tremendous amount of energy. Configuring a computer to automatically shut down the entire system, or individual components when not in use can have a noticeable impact on the bottom line.

    a. Power Management: User Defined/Max/Min. User Defined lets the user put in shutdown times for each individual component. Max provides settings for maximum energy savings and shuts the system down after a short period. The actual number of minutes can vary between brands of BIOS, but is generally between one and three minutes. Min generally sets the shutdown for all components at 30 minutes.

    b. PM Control by APM: Yes/No. Stands for Power Management by Advanced Power Management. APM is a Microsoft/Intel software implementation of power management and turns control over to the operating system.

    c. Video Suspend Option: Always On/Suspend->off/All Modes ->off. Different modes are Suspend, Standby, and Hibernation (on notebooks). Determines which mode the system will go into when the configured time of inactivity has elapsed.

    d. Video Off Method: Blank Screen/V/H Screen +Blank/DPMS Support. Blank Screen only blanks the screen. V/H Screen +Blank will turn off the V-Synch and H-Synch signals traveling between the video card and the monitor as well as blanking the monitor. Display Power

Management System is a software controlled method, that—if supported by the monitor—allows the operating system to establish values.

   e. Modem Uses IRQ: N/A or a listing of IRQ Settings. On a system that supports Wake on Modem, the IRQ of the modem needs to be configured here in order for the service to work.

   f. Soft-off By Pwr Button: Instant-off/Delay/Standby. Determines the effect of pressing the power button. Instant-off immediately turns the system off. Delay requires the user to hold the button in for at least four to six seconds before the system will shut down. Standby allows the user to press the button briefly to put the system into standby or to hold it in four to six seconds to shut the system off.

   g. State After Power Failure: Off/On. If set to off, when power is restored, the system will remain off. When set to on, it will reboot.

   h. Wakeup Events: Various settings.

      i. VGA: Off/On. If set to On a signal from the VGA card can wake the system.

      ii. LPT and COM: None/LPT/COM/LPT-COM. None prevents a signal from either LPT or COM from waking the system. The other three allow the user to set either LPT, COM, or both LPT and COM as signals that will wake it.

      iii. HDD and FDD: On/Off. Activity from either of these drives will wake the system when set to On.

      iv. PCI Master: On/Off. PCI Master refers to any device on the PCI bus that can initiate a data/exchange sequence. Data coming in from one of these devices will wake the system when set to On.

      v. Power on by PCI Card: On/Off. Allows incoming data from a PCI card to activate the system.

      vi. Wake on LAN/RING: On/Off. When enabled, allows either the modem or the NIC to activate the system.

      vii. RTC Alarm Resume: On/Off. When set to On, allows the Real Time Clock to wake the system. This will cause the next two values to become configurable.

         1. Date (of month): 1–31. The system will automatically activate each month on the date set.

         2. Resume Time: (hh:mm:ss). The exact time at which the system will resume. If a day is set in the Date field, the system will resume at that time on that date, each month. If no date is set, the system will wake up at that time every day.

      viii. Primary INTR: On/Off. Allows enabled IRQ channels to activate the system.

      ix. IRQs Activity Monitoring: Press Enter. This is where you enable or disable IRQs for the previous setting.

11. The next section is entitled PnP/PCI Configurations. This can be a handy part of the BIOS to understand when you have an adapter card that won't behave. Nothing in here will prevent your system from being usable if incorrectly configured. But a wrong setting might make a particular device disappear from the system.

   a. Reset Configuration Data: Disabled/Enabled. This forces the Extended Systems Configuration Data (ESCD) to be rebuilt from scratch. During the POST that follows the enabling of this option, all Plug 'n Play devices will be forced to relinquish their assigned resources and new allocations will be assigned based on the now-current configuration. This option should be set to Enabled any time changes in the remaining fields on this page are made. With most (if not all) brands of BIOS, this is one parameter that will reset itself to "Disabled" once the reconfiguration has been completed.

   b. Resources Controlled By: Auto(ESCD)/User. When set to Auto(ESCD), Plug 'n Play manages all resources. When set to User the following setting will be enabled.

   c. IRQ Resources: Press Enter. All available IRQs, and with certain brands of BIOS, the DMA channels as well, will appear in a list. The options for each entry are PCI Device or Reserved. Some version use ISA in place of Reserved. If set to PCI Device, that resource is kept available to Plug 'n Play. If not, it is removed from the available resource list and a non–Plug 'n Play device won't have to compete for it (and usually lose).

d. PCI/VGA Palette Snoop: Disabled/Enabled, Allows Video adapters to directly access RAM looking for video information. Unless you're using a PCI video card, this should be disabled.

e. Assign IRQ for VGA: Enabled/Disabled. Most modern VGA cards require an IRQ and therefore this needs to be enabled.

f. Assign IRQ for USB: Enabled/Disabled. If you do not use USB devices, there is no point in tying up the IRQ assigned to the USB hub on your machine. However, if this is disabled and you attempt to install a USB device, it won't be recognized.

g. PCI Latency Timer CLK: 0–255. Sets the number of FSB clock cycles that a PCI Master device can maintain control of the PCI bus. Setting this number too high takes clock cycles away from the CPU. Setting it too low can impede PCI I/O operations.

h. PIRQ_0 User IRQ: None/0-15. Configurations for Programmable Interrupts. Unless you *really* know what you're doing, this is not a setting you want to play with.

i. The next three settings are the same as above for PIRQ_1 through PIRQ_3.

12. Load Failsafe Defaults: Y/N. Okay, you messed around with some advanced chipset parameters I warned you about and now your system won't boot. Remember earlier I mentioned I'd show you how to revert to factory defaults. In this version of BIOS, there are actually two collections of default settings. Failsafe Defaults is the setting to use when all else fails. It disables all but the minimum configuration settings required to get the system to boot.

13. Load Optimized Defaults: Y/N. As with the previous setting, this loads a collection of default settings, but instead of the bare minimum settings required to boot, the Optimized Defaults are the settings designed for the greatest efficiency of the motherboard. This is the default setting you should always try first if playing around in the BIOS has rendered your system unbootable.

14. Set Password: Opens a blank field into which you can type a password. The security setting I discussed earlier determines whether the password applies to booting the system or to entering the CMOS Setup program.

15. Save and Exit Setup: Y/N. Y saves all the configuration changes you've made in your session, exits setup, and reboots the machine.

16. Discard Changes and Exit Setup: Y/N. Throws out all the changes you made and reboots the machine back to the way it was before you started playing around.

Select Discard Changes and Exit Setup, press <Enter> and let your system reboot. You're finished with this exercise. (Whew!)

Exercise 1 Review

1. Using what you learned from the above exercises and from your textbook, explain why changing a few settings in the Advanced BIOS Settings is unlikely to harm your computer, whereas changes in Advanced Chipset Settings may prevent your system from booting.

2. You've just made several changes in your BIOS settings and now the system won't boot. What are your options?

3. When trying to fine-tune a system, why do you think seasoned technicians always follow the rule of thumb that states, "Make only one change at a time"?

4. Which menu would you most likely open if you wanted to check how your system was configured for RAS/CAS Delay?

5. A user in your company has left without notice and password encoded the system they were using before their untimely departure? How are you going to get back into that system?

EXERCISE 2: BACKING UP THE CMOS

Well, you can see that in a finely tuned system, there can be quite a number of changes made in Setup. And I'm sure that it's safe to assume that six months from now, after you've changed your battery and discover that your CMOS has been wiped clean you will remember every change you made and precisely what those changes were, right? If you can do that, can I talk to you about working with me on my next book?

What we want is a safe way to back up those settings once we've made them. Notice that nowhere in any of the above sections were you offered an opportunity to do a CMOS backup. With a couple of notable exceptions (such as Compaq), CMOS backup is not an option. So you have two choices when it comes to backing up your CMOS. You can either record every change you make on a sheet of paper and hope you don't lose that paper between now and the time you need it: or you can use one of the several CMOS backup utilities available. These utilities range from free to relatively expensive. Because I'm notoriously cheap, I'm going to show you one of the freebies that I stumbled across that hasn't failed me yet. It's called CMOSBAK. EXE and is available at http://www.mwgraves.com.

When you first download this utility, it's going to be in zipped form, so you'll need an unzipping utility to expand it. I use Ultimate Zip, another freeware utility available for download on the above-mentioned site. Assuming that you haven't downloaded either, getting a useful rendition of CMOSBAK will require you to unzip the program and run the installation program.

Exercise 2a: Running CMOSBAK

Now that CMOSBAK is added to our diskette, we are ready to back up the CMOS on your system.

1. Insert the Technician's Boot Diskette into the floppy drive and start your machine. Once again, it will boot to the A: prompt.

2. From the A: prompt, type CMOSBAK. You'll get a screen like the one seen in **Figure L3-2**.

3. Unless you have a very old machine, select the option to Backup 128-byte Extended CMOS. Even if you're wrong, you won't do any harm. You'll have to use your Down Arrow <> on your keyboard to select this option. The mouse won't be working at this point.

4. Press the <Enter> key and in a second or less, a message will tell you that your CMOS has been successfully backed up.

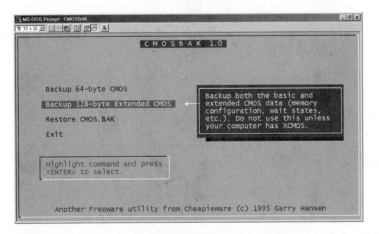

Figure L3-2   The CMOSBAK utility is a simple command-prompt utility that makes it easy to back up CMOS settings to a floppy diskette.

Exercise 2b: Restoring the CMOS

That was easy, wasn't it? Now let's see how to put our systems back to the way we had it. But we actually want to see that something really happened, don't we? So let's make some changes in the CMOS before we use the Restore function of CMOSBAK.

1. Remove the Technician's Boot Diskette from the floppy drive and restart your machine. This time you want to press the appropriate key sequence to enter the Setup program.

2. Navigate to the Boot Sequence in your CMOS and rearrange the order of the sequence. Record your changes on a sheet of paper.

3. Now find the settings for the serial and parallel ports and (if you BIOS supports making this change) set the COM and LPT settings to different settings. Record your changes.

4. Save your changes and exit. As the machine reboots, re-enter the Setup program and verify that your changes stuck.

5. Insert the Technician's Boot Diskette into Drive A: and restart the machine.

6. From the A: prompt type CMOSBAK.

7. Select the Restore CMOS.BAK option. In a second or two, it will inform you if the restore was successful. Remove the diskette and reboot the machine, once again entering the Setup program.

8. Review the changes you made and verify that they are back to their original settings.

Exercise 2 Review

1. What is the purpose of backing up the CMOS after achieving the optimum configuration?

2. One of the shortcomings of CMOSBAK is that a single diskette can only back up the CMOS settings for a single computer. Based on what you saw during the Restore exercise, explain why this is so.

3. Why doesn't the mouse work while running the CMOSBAK utility?

4

PERFORMING A BIOS UPGRADE

Performing a standard BIOS upgrade is one of those procedures that sometimes send chills up the spine of even a veteran technician. Although there are good reasons for that, there really is no reason to fear a BIOS upgrade. It's just one more task the IT specialist has to perform. As long as you are careful and systematic in your approach—and as long as nature doesn't curse you with a power outage halfway through the process—there will be no problems.

Although the vast majority of BIOS upgrades these days are of the Flash BIOS variety, there comes a time when you actually have to perform a physical BIOS upgrade. Therefore, this is a two-part lab. In part 1, you will perform a Flash upgrade, and in part 2, you'll actually replace the BIOS chip. This is where you actually get to use some of those tools that came in your toolkit.

EXERCISE 1: BEFORE THE UPGRADE

In the textbook, I mentioned that a BIOS upgrade should only be performed when there is a good reason. Those reasons might include adding support for new hardware, fixing a bug in an earlier BIOS version, or adding new capabilities to the system that the old BIOS doesn't support. A *wrong* reason would be, "It's newer, so it must be better." An old adage that I learned from my grandfather comes into play here. *If it ain't broke, don't fix it.* This lab assumes it is *broke*, even if it *ain't*. (My editor is going to have a field day with this paragraph!) In any case, whether you're flashing a new BIOS or performing a physical swap of chips, there are a few preliminary steps you need to take. Your instructor can decide which of these steps are necessary within the framework of this lab, but in the real world, you should do the following before messing around with the BIOS of any server:

1. Schedule the upgrade for a time when it will least affect the users on the network. (Because this is a lab, now would be good enough.)

2. Make sure that you have all the essential materials. For doing a flash upgrade, be certain that you have the flash utility, the BIOS data file, and most likely a bootable floppy diskette to put them both on.

3. Read any documentation the manufacturer provides with your new BIOS. There might be some quirks specific to your installation that you want to know *before* you learn about them the hard way.

4. Perform a full backup of the server. Until you've turned a SQL server into a doorstop by frying a motherboard with static discharge, you don't really think about what a critical step this is.

5. Record all custom CMOS settings before installing the new BIOS. The new one is going to come with factory defaults. A utility such as CMOS Backup (available at *http://www.mwgraves.com*) is useful for that.

6. Test the upgrade on a non-critical server before rolling the upgrade out on a mission-critical network.

Exercise 1 Review

1. What are the two files you need in order to perform a flash upgrade?

2. Why is it so necessary to perform a backup of the server is you're not doing anything to the hard disk system?

EXERCISE 2: THE FLASH BIOS UPGRADE

As with any upgrade, the procedure can be broken down into three stages. Stage one is preparation, which is where you make sure everything is ready for you to be able to complete the process from start to finish without interruption. Stage two is the actual upgrade process, and the final stage is configuration, testing, and documentation.

Stage One: Preparing for the Upgrade

1. Make sure there is really a *reason* for what you're doing. Check the current version of BIOS running on your machine to verify that you're not already running the most recent version. There are two ways to go about this.

   a. The first is to restart your computer. One of the first screens to appear lists the brand, version, and copyright date of the system BIOS. Because most of us can't read fast enough to extract all of that information in the three-quarters of a second they give you, now would be a good time to use the pause/break key on your keyboard. You will get a screen like the one in **Figure L4-1**.

   b. Another way is to use a simple utility, such as Bios Agent. This simple program can be downloaded from the author's Web site at *http://www.mwgraves.com* or from *http://www.mrbios.com*. This program is much more informative and does not require that you restart the computer. **Figure L4-2** shows a screen from BIOS Agent.

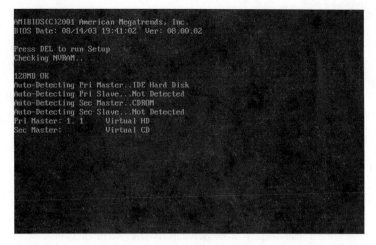

Figure L4-1 Unless a manufacturer's splash screen covers it, your BIOS information is clearly visible as the first thing you see at bootup.

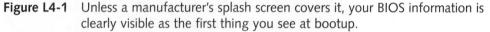

Figure L4-2 BIOS Agent provides much more information than just the version and copyright date.

2. Check with your manufacturer to see what the most recent version of your system's BIOS is. The vast majority of system and motherboard manufacturers provide not only the most recent BIOS version, but older ones as well in the event that you need to backtrack to an earlier version for any reason. There are essentially three ways to upgrade your BIOS.

   a. Some motherboards support a ROM-embedded flash utility. If this is the case with your motherboard, this is the best way to go. To upgrade the BIOS in this manner, enter the CMOS Setup in the conventional way (usually by pressing the Delete key). Then one of the options will be to Flash Your BIOS.

   b. Many manufacturers have finally acknowledged the passing of MS-DOS (some industries are slower than others in saying goodbye to a dead relative, no matter how little they cared for that relative). As a result, they now offer Windows-based BIOS upgrades.

c. The old standby DOS-based utility is the one that (almost) always works, regardless of the brand of motherboard or version of BIOS. I say "almost" because it does require that you have a bootable floppy diskette and a floppy drive. Floppy disk drives are disappearing from servers and other machines at a rapid rate. I'm going out on a limb with this lab and assuming that most educational institutions have access to machines with floppy drives and will base the lab on that. The other two methods are very similar once the flash utility is in play. I'll point out the differences in launching the utility.

3. Confirm the version of BIOS you wish to install and download it to your machine.

Stage Two: Performing the Upgrade

1. Create a bootable floppy diskette. This is much easier if you have an older WIN9x system available.

   a. If you are preparing a boot diskette from a WIN9x machine:

      i. Insert a blank diskette in the floppy disk drive. On the WIN9x box, open Windows Explorer. Right-click on the A drive and from the pop-up menu that appears, select Format. Be sure you're on Drive A and not Drive C.

      ii. If you are using a pre-formatted diskette, click on the Quick (erase) option under Format Type. Under Other Options, click on Copy system files. Click Start. When it has finished, you'll have the bare essentials for a bootable disk.

   b. If you're making a bootable disk from a disk image, do the following.

      i. Download the file BIOSBOOT.FIC from the Internet at *http://www.mwgraves.com*, along with the freeware application Floppy Image Creator (FIC). This is a freeware utility created by John Maher. Feel free to use it, but don't alter it or try to resell it for profit.

      ii. Extract FIC to a folder on any Windows machine and launch the program. It looks like the screen in **Figure L4-3**.

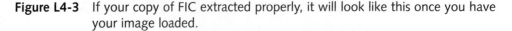

Figure L4-3   If your copy of FIC extracted properly, it will look like this once you have your image loaded.

iii. Click on the Restore Image Option

iv. Browse to the BIOSBOOT.FIC file. Place a blank, formatted 1.44MB floppy disk in your drive. Click on the button that says RESTORE Image To DRIVE A:. In about 30 seconds your disk will be created.

v. On the Internet, browse to the support site of your motherboard or computer manufacturer's technical support department. Locate and download the most recent version of BIOS for your system *and* the flash utility your manufacturer uses for transferring the new data files.

vi. If the BIOS utility and data files were compressed (as they most likely were), extract them to the new floppy disk you just created. In my case, the utility is called AFLASH.EXE and the data file is named XXXXX.XXX.

2. Insert your newly created floppy into the machine you're upgrading and restart the computer. Let it boot to the floppy.

3. Once the computer settles at the command prompt, type the command for your flash upgrade utility. I'll be typing AFLASH.

4. You will be prompted to select which version of BIOS you want to copy. Because you only have one choice, you probably won't find it a difficult one. Select the BIOS data file and carry on. During this procedure, the utility will completely wipe the BIOS chip clean and then do a block-by-block copy of the new code to the chip. That is why it is critical that you not power the machine down until it is finished. Whatever you do, from this point on, DO NOT SHUT OFF YOUR MACHINE!!!

Exercise 2 Review

1. What are the three ways of upgrading a flash BIOS that are used by different manufacturers?

2. What are the two files you need when flashing a BIOS from the floppy drive?

3. Why does losing power to your machine during the flash have such a disastrous effect?

EXERCISE 3: SWAPPING OUT A BIOS CHIP

In general, it should never be necessary to physically change a BIOS chip on newer machines. For several years, all systems have shipped with flash BIOS. Still, if you are one of the unlucky few to have your power fail halfway through an upgrade, you might find yourself in that position. This exercise will prevent you from being totally unprepared.

Stage One: Preparing for the Upgrade

1. As with the flash upgrade, your first step is to determine the make and version of your current motherboard/BIOS combination. Your best source for that information is the utility we used above.

2. When ordering a new BIOS chip, you want to replace it with the correct one. On the chip is a long number called the *BIOS identification string*. This tells the manufacturer the make, model, and version of your BIOS chip. When they ship you the new chip, it is very likely that you will have to flash it to the most recent version. Aren't you glad you did the first exercise now?

    i. An AMI BIOS string looks like 62-0113-zz6455-01234599-101097-AMIS124-P, or some similar variation. On a motherboard older than 1991, it will look different. The four numbers following the Zs are the manufacturer's identification code.

    ii. An Award BIOS looks like 2C7LEF09C-00. The first five characters identify the motherboard's chipset. Characters six and seven identify the motherboard's manufacturer.

3. In the real world, this is the part where you sit back and wait for two or three days for the guy or gal with the delivery van to bring you a small package from your vendor. In our world, we're going to cheat and simply put back the chip we pulled out. Be careful: This is the machine you have to work with for the rest of the semester.

Stage Two: Performing the Surgery

1. As with any other work involving the inside of your computer, you must take care to protect the system from ESD. Ideally, you should be standing on an anti-static floor mat, the system should be sitting on an anti-static counter mat, and you should be wearing a properly grounded anti-static wrist strap.

2. Open the computer enclosure. This isn't a basic hardware course, so I'm not going into the various ways that manufacturers design their cases. If you can't figure it out, your instructor can help.

3. Locate the BIOS chips. It's the one that looks like **Figure L4-4**.

Figure L4-4   In most machines, the BIOS chip is easily identifiable by the manufacturer's logo splattered all over the label.

4. Position your chip extractor with the inverted teeth gripping the short edges of the chip as seen in **Figure L4-5**. Pull *straight* out. Do not wiggle it out or rock it back and forth. It is not a loose tooth and it is not a baby that you're trying to put to sleep. You may have to use a little elbow grease and pull firmly, but since you need to use this chip again, you don't want to bend any pins.

5. To reseat the chip back in its socket, place it into the chip inserter as seen in **Figure L4-6**. Carefully position the pins over the holes and, using the plunger, gently press the chip into the socket. Rotate the chip inserter 90 degrees and press the chip down until it is fully seated.

6. Close the case.

Exercise 3 Review

1. What is the number that identifies the manufacturer and BIOS version called?

2. What is the most critical precaution you can take prior to changing out the BIOS chip in your machine?

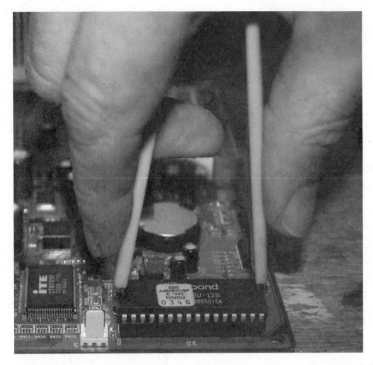

Figure L4-5 Make sure the teeth on your chip extractor are fully positioned beneath the chip before pulling. Ceramic is easier to crack than you might think.

Figure L4-6 Proper use of a chip inserter makes installing a new chip much easier.

EXERCISE 4: AFTER THE UPGRADE

The following is a checklist of things to do more than it is an actual exercise. Once the upgrade is finished, you need to return to your original status quo, as much as possible. Perform the following steps to make sure the upgrade was truly successful.

1. Restore any custom CMOS settings. If you used CMOS Backup, it should be easy enough to restore your settings as long as the BIOS versions aren't so drastically different as to make the settings incompatible.

2. Test all hardware devices attached to the system to assure that they all work properly.

3. Run a new baseline to make sure that the "upgrade" didn't have negative effects on performance.

5

INSTALLING IDE DEVICES

CompTIA Objectives Covered in this Lab

1.2 Identify basic procedures for adding and removing field replaceable modules for both desktop and portable systems.

1.5 Identify proper procedures for installing and configuring IDE/EIDE devices.

1.8 Identify hardware methods of upgrading system performance, procedures for replacing basic subsystem components, unique components and when to use them.

2.1 Identify common symptoms and problems associated with each module and how to troubleshoot and isolate the problems.

As a technician, one of the most common tasks a technician you'll find yourself doing is installing a new drive. You are always adding or replacing hard drives, CD burners, DVD drives, and so on. For the most part, it's a straightforward procedure. However, you will occasionally encounter a few pitfalls. Knowledge is the key to avoiding those pitfalls. In this lab, we'll need:

- The Lab Computer

- An IDE hard disk drive

- An IDE optical drive (CD, CD-RW, or DVD)

- A 2-connector IDE cable (preferably an older-style 40-conductor, non–cable-select version)

- The toolkit

Exercise 1: Replacing a Hard Drive

When replacing a hard drive, one of the first things you need to do is take out the old one. As I pointed out in Lab 3, different manufacturers have different methods for mounting hard drives in a system. So once again, I'll point out the most common. All of these methods involve some form of dedicated drive bay in which the drive resides.

1. Standard Drive Bays. The vast majority of designs involve a standard drive bay. When you open the case, you will see where the external drives are installed. Directly below these are two or more 3.5" drive bays. They may or may not be removable. One is external for the floppy disk drive. There may one or more additional externally accessible bays for adding tape drives or Zip drives. The ones we're interested in are the ones with no access to the outside world. If the drive bays are removable, there will be either a screw affixing the cage to the 5.25" external bays above it, one or two screws affixing it to the front of the frame, or it may simply rotate upward out of the case.

2. Front Panel Drive Bays. These are more commonly seen with micro-ATX mini-tower cases. The drive mounts vertically in a bay located on the inner surface of the front panel of the frame. Four screws hold the drive in place. To access these screws, you must remove the front plastic (and you'll need to check with the specific manufacturer on how that is done).

3. Power Supply Drive Bays. These were common in older designs but are no longer popular because of the heat generated by today's higher-rpm drives. One or more 3.5" drive bays were located directly beneath the power supply, and in some cases, one of the drives was actually affixed to the power supply.

The above list doesn't represent every possibility, but it certainly represents the vast majority of machines you're likely to encounter today. Once you've determined which design you have, we can proceed to the removal process.

1. Remove the IDE and Molex cables from the drive. In smaller enclosures, it is best to remove it completely from the system and set it aside. It can get in the way. If the cables aren't keyed, make a note of which direction the #1 conductor on the cable is pointed. That is the pink or red wire on the ribbon cable. If you get it backward later, you won't do any damage, but the drives on that cable won't work!

2. If working with a removable drive bay, remove it. If not, make sure that both side panels are removed from the enclosure.

3. Remove the four screws affixing the drive to the cage. As you can see in **Figures L5–1** and **L5–2**, these screws may be located on the sides of the drive or on the base. All hard drives are designed to be mounted either way.

4. Slide the drive out of the bay.

Figure L5-1   In this illustration, you can clearly see the screw holes on the sides of the drive used for mounting it into the system. You also see the 40-pin connector, the power socket, and the master/slave jumpers if you look closely enough (and if reproduction holds up).

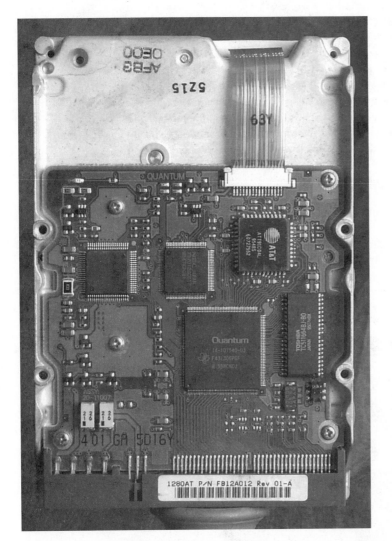

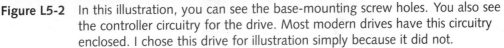

Figure L5-2   In this illustration, you can see the base-mounting screw holes. You also see the controller circuitry for the drive. Most modern drives have this circuitry enclosed. I chose this drive for illustration simply because it did not.

Now that wasn't so hard now, was it? I'd like to say that replacing the new drive is simply a reversal of the above process. For the most part, it is. However, in the replacement procedure, we need to add a step.

Before installing the new drive into the system, make sure that the master/slave jumpers are set properly. It is frustrating to spend several minutes fighting with a poorly designed micro-ATX enclosure mounting the drives only to find out that your new drive isn't being recognized by the system. In addition, it's a good idea to attach the IDE cables to the drive while it's still outside the system and you have plenty of room to work.

When working with removable drive bays, it's a good idea to attach the IDE cables before you put the drives back into the case. You have more room to work. Also, if you're working with 80-conductor cables—which is most likely to be the case on any system using newer drives—you have a couple of other things to consider. The 80-conductor cables like the one in **Figure L5-3** are cable-select by default. The master drive will go on the end connector and the slave onto the middle one. You want to put the master drive in the top bay and the slave beneath it if you're installing two drives. Otherwise, you'll end up having to twist your cable around to make it work properly. Over time, ribbon cables that have been twisted to extreme angles can fail due to metal fatigue in the 24-awg wires used in their design.

As you're sliding the drive into the bay, before it's all the way back into the enclosure and while you still have some room in which to manipulate your fingers, now is the time to attach the Molex connectors. In the vast majority of enclosures, once the drive is in place, you have one or two inches between the back of the drive and the power supply. If your hands are as big as mine, or if you suffer from Coordination Deficiency Syndrome (CDS), as I do, then trying to attach the Molex after the drive is in place can result in problems.

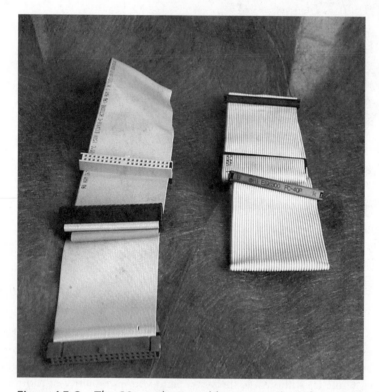

Figure L5-3   The 80-conductor cable seen on the left is cable-select by default. The 40-conductor cables, like the one on the right, may be cable-select. If a notch has been clipped from the section between the middle and end conductors on the 28th wire, you know it is cable-select. However, if the manufacturer simply didn't attach that wire to the connector you can't tell just by looking.

Don't just replace the drive back in your machine, however. Pull the shunt off the jumper (Don't drop it! Manufacturers somehow know what color of carpet you're working over and always make the shunt the same color.) and swap drives with another classmate. Now you can install your new drive, making sure that it is properly jumpered for your system. If you're using the older non-cable-select 40-conductor cables as I suggested in the introduction to this lab, you're going to have to figure out which setting to use.

Exercise 1 Review

1. You've just opened the enclosure and there are no apparent internal drive bays for a hard disk. Where else might the manufacturer have hidden the drive?

2. What additional step do you commonly have to perform in order to remove hard disks that have been attached to the front of the frame?

3. What is the name of the cable commonly used to provide power to the hard drive?

4. What are the two locations for screw holes on 3.5" hard drives?

5. What are the three possible jumper settings for an IDE drive?

5

EXERCISE 2: INSTALLING MULTIPLE DRIVES ON A SINGLE IDE PORT

In this exercise, we will make two different IDE devices coexist on the same IDE port using a two-device cable. To make it more of a challenge, we'll divide the class into two sections. You'll see why in a few minutes.

1. Open your computer and remove the hard drive and the CD-ROM. Also, pull the IDE cable(s). If the systems used in your class had each device on a separate single-channel cable, these cables should be set aside and a cable designed to support two devices should be substituted.

2. Pull the shunts from the jumpers of both drives.

3. Take both drives and their shunts over to a person in the other section and trade with them.

4. Install their drives into your system, after making sure both drives are jumpered properly.

Once you have installed the drives and confirmed that they are both working properly, reassemble your systems. You're finished with this lab.

Some IDE Troubleshooting Tips

IDE drives are fairly trouble-free in both installation and configuration. The advent of cable-select drives and cables makes it a simple matter of setting the jumper on each drive to cable-select and making sure your primary disk is on the end connector. A few things might get in the way of this working to your benefit. Among these are:

- Some drives need to be master drives on the channel. This might include primary boot drives on older systems, and some models of CD-RW. If these drives are configured to be a slave, they'll either not be recognized by the system, or will not function properly once the system has booted.

- If the device that needs to be the slave on the cable is positioned too far for you to attach the middle connector on the cable to that device and then loop the end connector down to the primary device, then you might have to put these devices on separate channels. A master device *cannot* be attached to the slave connector on a cable-select cable.

- If the IDE channel being used has been disabled in the CMOS, then you can tear your hair out trying to determine why you can't get a device to be recognized by the system. With many versions of BIOS, instead of telling you that the channel has been disabled, you simply seen the word NONE for devices on that channel. Change the setting to AUTO.

- Failure to attach the Molex connector to the drive: As amazing as it may sound, a hard drive can be compared to your refrigerator in that, if it doesn't have an available supply of electricity, it won't work.

- Reversing the IDE cable on either the drive or the motherboard connector. Not all IDE cables are keyed, and if your cable is plugged in backward, the drive won't be recognized. You won't hurt anything. But it won't work.

LAB SUMMARY

Now that you have had some hands-on experience with IDE devices, they won't even cause you to break a sweat once you're in the field. However, as we all know, if there is a possibility of something going wrong, it will. Sometimes what looks like a bad hard drive is actually a bad cable, or even a bad motherboard. So after you're replaced your drive and it still doesn't work, do the following:

- Double-check your jumpers. You don't want one drive set to cable select and the other to slave.

- Check your cable. If you have a cable select cable and the drive on the end is set to be a slave, it'll never be seen by the system. The drive at the end must be the master.

- Make sure all cables are properly seated and positioned in the socket. With larger ribbon cable connectors, it's easy to have one side not pushed all the way in. Also, not all IDE cables are keyed. When they're not, they are easy to plug in backward.

- Make sure the power cables are attached to the drives. I can't count the number of times I've been summoned by a student who said that their drive wasn't being recognized by the system, only to discover that the power cable wasn't plugged in. (Of course, *I've* never done that!)

6

WORKING WITH SCSI

CompTIA Objectives Covered in this Lab

1.2 Identify basic procedures for adding and removing field replaceable modules for both desktop and portable systems.

1.3 Identify available IRQs, DMAs, and I/O addresses and procedures for device installation and configuration.

1.4 Identify common peripheral ports, associated cabling and their connectors.

1.6 Identify proper procedures for installing and configuring SCSI devices.

For years now, the computing industry has accepted the fact that high-end workstations and servers need to be equipped with SCSI. The advent of technologies such as Serial ATA has slowed this tendency in workstations, but servers, for the most part, still use SCSI.

Newer implementations of SCSI, such as Fiber Channel Arbitrated Loop, are generally trouble-free and fairly automatic in their installation. Also, FCAL is usually installed and configured at the factory on most servers. However, older technologies such as Parallel SCSI still require a bit of knowledge on the part of the technician. Therefore, in these exercises, you will be installing and configuring a SCSI-II chain.

To complete these exercises, you will need at the minimum:

- The Student Computers, equipped with KB, monitor, and mouse

- A PCI SCSI host adapter

- A SCSI cable with a minimum of three device connectors, in addition to the connector for the controller

- A SCSI hard disk (two if possible)

- Any other secondary internal SCSI device (a tape drive or CD-ROM will be suitable)

- The manuals for the SCSI devices and controller

In the following exercises, I will be working with 50-pin SCSI. If you purchased your components new, they are more likely to be either 68- or 80-pin devices and cables.

EXERCISE 1a: Installing the Host Adapter

The first thing you need to do is install the host adapter (**Figure L6-1**). For these labs, I have specified that the classrooms be equipped with SCSI expansion cards. However, it should be noted that many high-end motherboards are equipped with on-board SCSI and this step would only be necessary in the event that a second SCSI chain was required.

Figure L6-1   A SCSI host adapter will be equipped with at least one internal connector for a SCSI cable. Most adaptors, such as this Adaptec 2940AU, are also equipped with a connector for hooking up external devices.

1. Examine the manual for the host adapter and see if configuration settings are performed via a setup program or if there are jumpers or dipswitches involved. A Plug 'n Play host adapter will most likely not have any manual settings for IRQ and/or I/O channel. But there may be manual settings for terminating the adapter and for setting its device ID. On most (if not all) newer devices, even these settings are accomplished in the setup program. If there are jumpers to be set, now is the time to set them.

2. Open the case and locate a free expansion slot.

3. Carefully insert the host adapter into the slot and tighten down the screw that affixes the adapter to the backplane.

4. Attach the SCSI cable (**Figure L6-2**) to the internal connector. If using two-channel adapters, it is best to use Channel A. You are now ready to tackle the devices.

Exercise 1b: Installing the SCSI Devices

In the physical installation of SCSI devices, there are few differences between those devices and the IDE devices you installed in Lab Four. There are some critical differences in configuration and cabling.

1. Examine the manual for the device to see how Device IDs are set for the particular device. The Seagate Barracuda seen in **Figure L6-3** has a series of jumpers. As the illustration indicates, the smaller block is for terminating the drive and the larger one is for various other settings. As far as other models of drive are concerned, the variety of options is as wide as the variety of devices. That is why you need the manual.

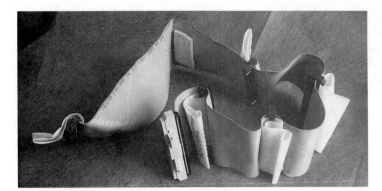

6

Figure L6-2   This particular cable is designed for four devices in addition to the host adapter. This is a deluxe cable in two respects. First, each connector is equipped with pull loops for removing it from the device later. Second, on the end of the cable, the cable itself is terminated, so there is no concern about terminating individual devices. I just make sure they are *not* terminated.

2. Set each of the devices that you're installing to a different device ID. If using a terminated SCSI cable, such as the one in **Figure L6-2**, all devices should be unterminated. If the cable is not terminated, the last device on the chain needs to be terminated. Once again, the methods for terminating devices vary. In the hard disk illustrated in **Figure L6-3**, jumpers are used. Other methods include a terminating resistor that is plugged into a socket and software-configurable termination. In the latter case, the device is configured in the setup program.

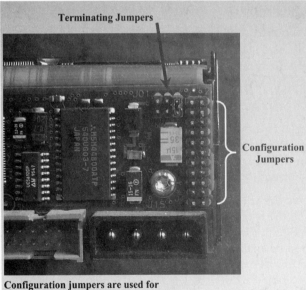

Terminating Jumpers

Configuration Jumpers

Configuration jumpers are used for setting device IDs and for other settings, including parity, motor startup delay and others

Figure L6-3   On this Seagate Barracuda, Device IDs and other settings are made manually with these jumpers.

3. Once the device ID and termination is properly configured, install the devices in the appropriate drive bay and attach the cables. The Molex cable is no different from that of the IDE devices you installed. However, unlike IDE devices, plugging a SCSI cable in backwards can damage or destroy the device and/or the host adapter. On the 68- and 80-pin cables, this is not an issue, because both cables use D-shell connectors and only plug in one way. On the 50-conductor cables and connectors, *most* are keyed to prevent this from happening. If the cable is not keyed, make sure that the colored conductor on the ribbon cable is lined up to pin number 1.

4. Another thing to consider is that most computers have an LED disk activity light on the front panel. If you disconnect the cable from the LED connector on the motherboard and connect it to the LED connector on the host adapter, the LED on the front panel of the computer will light whenever there is activity on the SCSI bus. That way, regardless of which hard drive is active, the LED will flicker.

Exercise 1c: SCSI Setup

Once the devices are installed, it's time to check your setup. When you initially turn on the system after installing a SCSI host adapter, if the adapter is successfully recognized by the system, you'll see some changes in your POST. Immediately after the conventional POST to which you grew accustomed, a message will appear telling you that the BIOS for your SCSI adapter was successfully loaded. You will also be prompted to press a specific key to enter Setup. This is not the same setup we looked at in Lab Nine. This is the SCSI Setup.

Immediately after this prompt, the SCSI host adapter will scan the SCSI bus looking for all installed devices. If you have properly configured the devices you installed, each on a different device ID, then the adapter should have no trouble identifying the devices and reporting the device ID that they have claimed. In this case, there is really no reason to enter the SCSI setup. But what fun would that be, and how could I lead you on a tour of what you can accomplish in the setup program?

Since different folks will be using different setup programs, I am not going to clutter this section with screen shots that might be confusing to many. Simply start your setup program and look for the following settings. Note that not all setup programs contain the same settings, but most should have the ones discussed in the following section.

1. SCSI Bus Interface: Allows the user to configure IRQ and decide whether to employ parity checking.

2. Boot Options: Determines whether to boot from the SCSI bus, and if so, which device ID identifies the boot disk. On many brands, this is also where Logical Unit Numbers (LUN) are configured for multiple devices on the same device ID. This will tell the host adapter to treat all devices with the same device ID, but with unique LUNs, as a single device.

3. SCSI Device Configuration: Allows the user to configure maximum transfer rate for a specific device, enable write-back cache, tell the host adapter whether the device can negotiate bus width (such as Wide SCSI or Fast/Wide SCSI). On many brands, there will be an additional setting for configuring LUNs. This setting must be enabled for multiple devices to be span multiple LUNs on a single device ID. The default setting is usually disabled. Also, in many brands, you can dictate whether you want the SCSI scan to be a part of your BIOS scan. Unless you have a good reason for not doing this, I recommend you leave this setting at the default, which is enabled.

4. Advanced Configuration Options: Not all adapters will have these settings.
   a. SCAM Support: Newer adapters use a protocol known as SCSI Configuration Automatically (SCAM). If enabled, this gives Plug 'n Play capability to the SCSI Bus. If the devices also support SCAM, then the host adapter automatically assigns device IDs.
   b. Reset SCSI Bus at IC Initialization: During startup, or after a hard reset, the host adapter will automatically issue a RESET command to all devices on the bus.
   c. Support Removable Disks Under BIOS as Fixed Disks: provides three options.
      i. Boot Only: A removable media drive that has been designated as a boot device will be treated as though it were a hard disk.

ii. All Disks: All removable media will be treated as though it were a hard disk.

iii. Disabled: No removable media will be treated as though it were a hard disk.

d. Display <Ctrl-A> Message During BIOS Initialization: This message may vary from brand to brand, but it lets the user determine whether the SCSI BIOS will issue a prompt as to what key sequence to press in order to enter SCSI BIOS Setup.

There are likely other settings visible as well. But these are the ones that are universally important.

LAB SUMMARY

If you think this was bad, you should have seen what technicians went through in the old days of SCSI. Back then, it wasn't uncommon for the host adapter from one manufacturer to refuse to recognize devices from another. All the settings were manually configured! As time goes on, it's going to get even easier. Most serial SCSI devices are auto-configuring and require little or no attention from the technician. Still, when it comes time to configure that RAID array, it's nice to know that you have some idea of what you're doing.

Lab 6 Review

1. What different settings might have to be manually configured on an older host adapter?

2. What is one critical difference between hooking the ribbon cable up to a SCSI device and hooking one up to an IDE device?

3. You have just installed a new SCSI chain and nothing works. During POST and in Windows Device Manager, the host adapter is recognized. What is a likely reason for failure?

4. You have just installed a new device on an existing SCSI chain. All the old devices still work, but the new device is not recognized. What are two things that might cause this problem?

5. How would you configure three different hard drives to work as a single array?

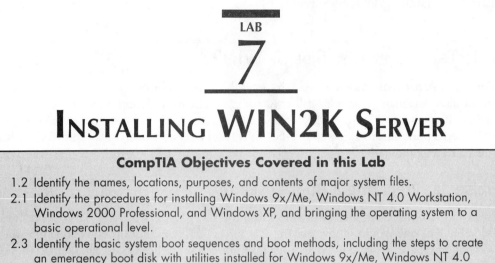

LAB
7
INSTALLING WIN2K SERVER

CompTIA Objectives Covered in this Lab

1.2 Identify the names, locations, purposes, and contents of major system files.

2.1 Identify the procedures for installing Windows 9x/Me, Windows NT 4.0 Workstation, Windows 2000 Professional, and Windows XP, and bringing the operating system to a basic operational level.

2.3 Identify the basic system boot sequences and boot methods, including the steps to create an emergency boot disk with utilities installed for Windows 9x/Me, Windows NT 4.0 Workstation, Windows 2000 Professional, and Windows XP.

Although we are not entirely finished with hardware yet, before we go any further, it is time to put an operating system (OS) onto the computer. It will be essential for the remaining labs.

There are those who argue that installing an operating system (OS) is not a function of a network administrator. Those are the people who either have the luxury of an extremely large and diverse staff, or simply have not spent enough time in the real world. There will come a time when you will have to install an OS on a new system or completely rebuild an existing one.

In the following exercises, we will be installing Windows 2000 Professional. In order to complete the exercises we will need to use the following items:

- The Student Workstations

- Windows 2000 Server CDs for each computer

- Four blank, formatted 1.44MB floppy diskettes

EXERCISE 1: THE FLOPPY DISK SIDE OF WIN2K

For the most part, Microsoft has tried to forget the floppy drive ever existed. However, it has made concessions to the fact that many machines still exist today that require the services of the floppy disk drive to boot a system. If you are trying to install WIN2K onto a system that is so old that it won't boot to a CD-ROM, you will need a boot disk to access the WIN2K CD and a set of four installation disks to install the OS. You also need a new computer.

Exercise 1a: Preparing a Boot Diskette

Most modern machines will easily boot from the CD-ROM drive, and because the Windows 2000 CD is a bootable CD, one would simply put the CD in the drive and boot the machine. For the next two exercises, we will attack a worst-case scenario. Our machine refuses to boot from the CD, so we must use the 4-disk set of installation diskettes. Because this is a lab, we'll carry it a step further. Nobody knows where the setup diskettes are, so we need to make our own.

As if this writing, it is safe to say that most network environments still have a number of systems with Windows 98 installed. If this is not the case, you can download a boot image from http://www.mwgraves.com. To create a boot disk on a Windows 98 machine, open the Control Panel. This can be done by either right-clicking on My Computer and clicking Properties, and then double-clicking the Control Panel icon; or you can click on Start>Settings>Control Panel.

In Control Panel, double-click on Add/Remove Programs. The right-hand tab at the top says Startup Disk. Click on that tab, make sure that there is a blank, formatted high-density floppy diskette in the drive and click Create Disk. You now have the necessary tool for starting your computer.

If you happen to have a machine that does not have the .cab files installed, it will prompt you for the Windows 98 CD.

Exercise 1a Review:

1. Where in WIN98 is the Startup Disk creation utility located?
2. What size diskette is required to make this disk?

Exercise 1b: Creating the Windows 2000 Boot Disk Set

Using the boot diskette you just created (or were supplied), start your machine with the diskette in the drive. Select the option "Start computer with CD-ROM Support" and let the machine boot. If your machine will not boot the floppy, it is likely that your CMOS simply needs to be configured accordingly. Consult with your instructor for the appropriate methods for configuring the CMOS on your particular machine

Once the machine boots, it will tell you what drive letter it assigned to the CD-ROM drive. With the WIN98 Startup Diskette, assuming that there is only one hard drive, this is usually E because the startup diskette creates a virtual drive in memory onto which it copies certain files.

From this point, we will assume the CD-ROM to be Drive E. If this is not the case on your particular system, simply substitute the appropriate drive letter whenever Drive E is referenced. Now we're ready to begin installation.

1. Log on to the CD-ROM by typing E: <Enter>. At the E: Prompt, type CD bootdisk <Enter>.

Some schools are provided special versions of Windows 2000 for educational purposes. If you are using the 120-day Evaluation (For Educational Use) or the MSDN CD provided by Microsoft, the I386 directory may be a subdirectory buried elsewhere on the CD. If this is the case, your instructor will have the appropriate information

2. At the E:\bootdisk prompt, type makeboot <enter>. The screen shown in **Figure L7-1** will appear. Have four blank, formatted high-density floppy diskettes ready. Setup will then ask you to confirm the location of the files it needs (**Figure L7.2**). Press <Enter> to accept the default path. You will be prompted to enter what drive the diskette is in. Press the A key and make sure that one of the diskettes is in Drive A. This becomes your Installation Boot Diskette. Once this diskette is complete, you will be prompted to insert Diskettes 2, 3, and 4. To avoid confusion, label the diskettes as you go.

7

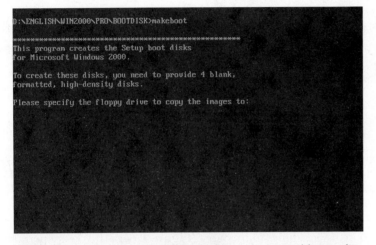

Figure L7-1   The MAKEBOOT utility is a command line utility.

Figure L7-2   This screen is merely confirming the path to the data that Setup detected. Press <Enter> to accept the default.

Exercise 1b Review

1. How many diskettes are needed for the WIN2K installation set?

2. Where is the utility that creates these disks located on the WIN2K Installation CD?

EXERCISE 2: INSTALLING WINDOWS 2000

Okay, now that we have created those installation diskettes, you're going to love the fact that I'm not going to use them in this lab. Save them for future use, but installing from diskettes is far too time consuming to fall within the constraints of a lab session. We'll boot from the CD and go from there.

1. Place the Installation CD into your CD-ROM drive and reboot the machine. The first screen to come up is a DOS screen (**Figure L7-3**) telling you that setup is inspecting your hardware configuration. This is NTDETECT at work.

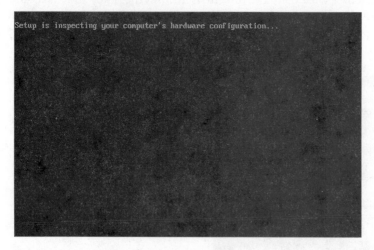

Setup is inspecting your computer's hardware configuration...

Figure L7-3   Setup's first task is to make sure you have the correct hardware configuration.

2. Next, Setup must copy some essential files to memory (**Figure L7-4**). (If you are performing this setup from the floppy disk set, you will be prompted for each diskette as it is needed.) This is known as the *text-based* portion of Setup.

Windows 2000 Setup

Setup is loading files (Locale-Specific Data)...

Figure L7-4   The first file copy isn't copying files to your hard disk, but rather to RAM. The hard disk hasn't been formatted yet.

3. Once these files have been copied, a new screen will appear, similar to the one in **Figure L7-5**, giving you three options. Pressing the <Enter> key will begin a new installation of Windows. Pressing R allows you to repair an existing installation using the Emergency Repair Diskette (ERD), and F3 allows you to exit Setup without doing anything.

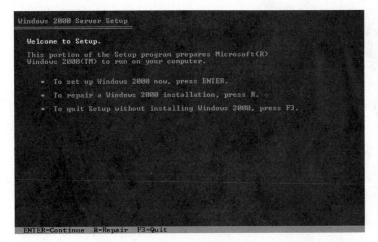

Figure L7-5   Now, you have the choice of performing a new installation, repairing an existing installation, or exiting setup. Note that in this illustration, I am installing Windows 2000 Server. Yours may say Windows 2003 Server. The installation process is the same.

4. Assuming you're installing your OS to a newly installed disk drive, you'll now see the screen shown in **Figure L7-6**. You will also see this screen if you are installing over an incompatible OS such as Unix or Linux. Press C to continue. This will initiate the WIN2K disk partitioning utility.

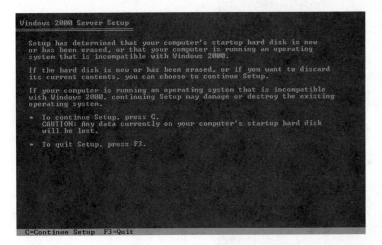

Figure L7-6   On a new or freshly FDISKED hard drive, or if you are replacing an OS such as Unix or Linux, this window advises you that you are about to wipe your drive.

5. Now read every single word of the licensing agreement that appears in **Figure L7-7**. It is about eight pages long, so give the slower readers time to absorb all of Microsoft's generous terms. Either that, or simply press <F8> to continue. If you don't agree, this is as far as you get and the rest of the class has to wait until you get caught up again.

6. Now it is time to create your primary partitions (**Figure L7-8**). Because of the nature of a later lab that appears in this manual, I don't want you to prepare your drive with just one partition. For now, create a partition of 2GB, onto which the OS will be installed. So press <C> to create a new partition.

7. In the next screen that appears (**Figure L7-9**), you will create your partitions. The default is to use the entire drive. In the bottom field, the number that is filled in represents total drive space. In order to replace that number, you must backspace to the beginning. Fill in the number 2048.

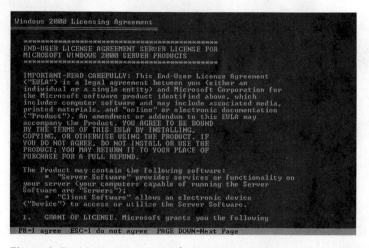

Figure L-7 You must accept the Licensing Agreement in order to continue.

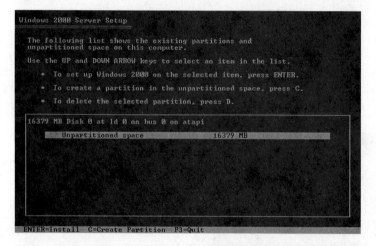

Figure L7-8 On a new drive, the first thing you must do is create the partitions.

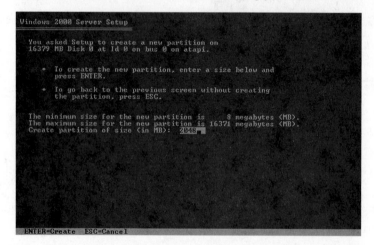

Figure L7-9 It isn't always a good idea to make your hard disk into a single partition. Put your OS and related utilities onto one partition, and then install your applications and store user data on separate partitions.

8. When you see the next screen (**Figure L7–10**) that asks you if you want to install your OS onto the newly created partition or into unformatted space, this may seem like a no-brainer. But in situations where you are installing a second OS onto the system, this is the point where Setup creates the information needed for your system to dual boot.

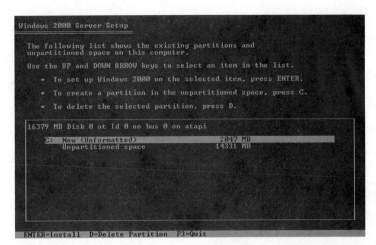

Figure L7-10   If you were installing WIN2K onto a previously partitioned disk with another existing OS, this screen would identify the file system installed and how much space was occupied by that file system.

9. Now sit back and wait while your partition is formatted. This generally takes long enough for a cup of coffee and donut while the class mingles in the break room discussing the football playoffs.

NOTE   During the initial formatting process, the hard drive will be formatted to FAT, even if you selected NTFS as your file system of choice. If you are creating a file system of 2GB or larger, it will automatically format the drive to FAT32. Any partition smaller than 2GB will be formatted in FAT16.

10. The next option (**Figure L7-11**) allows you to choose the file system you want to use on your new partition. Your choices are FAT or NFTS. FAT is a poor choice for many reasons. The one reason of biggest concern to you is that if you DO NOT choose NFTS you won't be able to do some of the later labs.

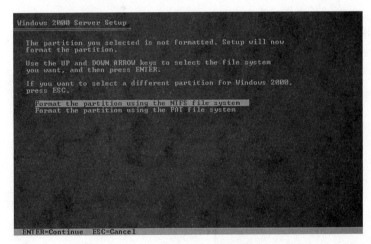

Figure L7-11   One of the bigger advantages of WIN2K over previous Windows versions was the NTFS file system. Unless there is a compelling reason not to do so, WIN2K computers should always be formatted to NTFS.

11. On reboot, you enter the graphical portion of the installation process. A screen with the Windows 2000 Professional logo will appear. At the bottom a progress bar labeled "Starting up" will appear.

12. After that, Setup will convert the drive to NFTS. This takes a minute or two. The computer will automatically reboot again.

13. Setup will now perform a thorough Plug 'n Play (PnP) scan (**Figure L7-12**), looking for any PnP devices and/or legacy devices previously installed on a prior OS (in the case of an upgrade). If your screen appears to flicker and Setup halts for a few minutes, this is normal. If Setup halts for an abnormally long time, it is probably hung and you will need to restart your machine again.

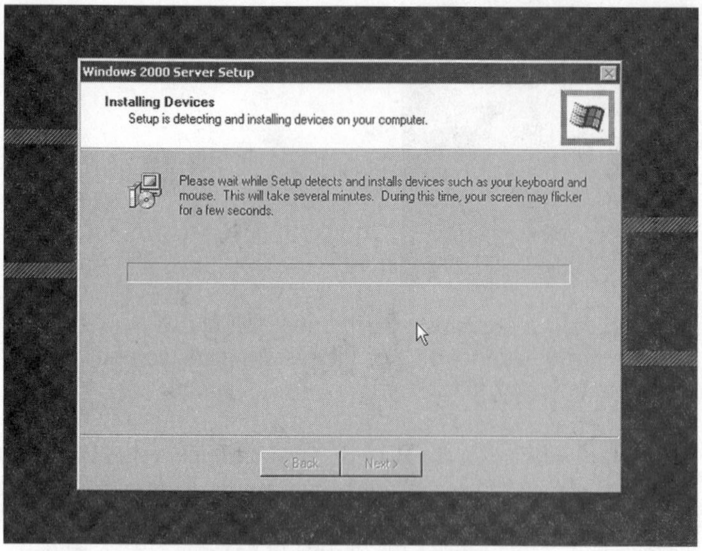

Figure L7-12   The Plug 'n Play scan detects your hardware and creates a list of device drivers to be installed. Contrary to what the screen says, not all devices are being installed at this point. But you do have mouse support now.

14. When this is finished, you'll have the opportunity to configure your regional settings (**Figure L7-13**). Generally, in the United States no changes need to be made here. For overseas users, it might be necessary to click the Customize button. Click Next and in the screen shown in **Figure L7-14**, type in your name and organization (organization is optional.)

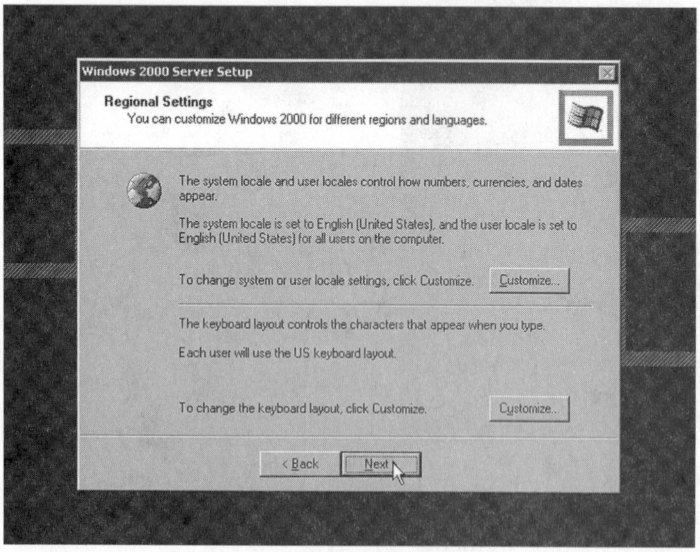

Figure L7-13   In the United States, it isn't generally necessary to make any changes to the Regional settings. But overseas users can change the currency settings as well as how numbers and dates are displayed.

15. Now it is time to type in the 25-digit CD key that shipped with the software. Type carefully, or you'll be doing it again.

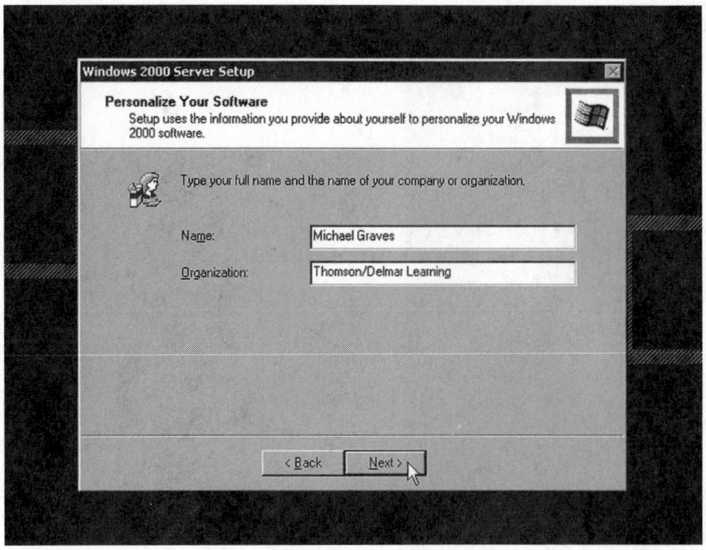

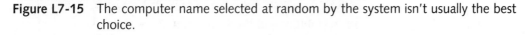

Figure L7-14   It isn't necessary to type an organization name, but setup won't continue until you type in a user name.

16. The following screen (**Figure L7-15**) will provide a suggested NetBIOS computer name. We won't be using their suggestion. Student machines will be named STUDENT1 through STU-DENT12 (or however many student machines there are in the classroom). Here is where the password is selected. For the password *all* students will simply use *password*. This will avoid the inevitable confusion when someone says, "I forgot my password."

Figure L7-15   The computer name selected at random by the system isn't usually the best choice.

17. Next you set the time and date (**Figure L7-16**) if it is incorrect and reset the time zone to your own. It will default to Pacific Standard.

18. Setup will now begin installing networking components, followed by Windows 2000 Components (**Figure L7-17**). Let everything install as per default.

7

Figure L7-16   Time and date display. Now you know what time and day it was when I wrote this lab. Send me a present on the anniversary.

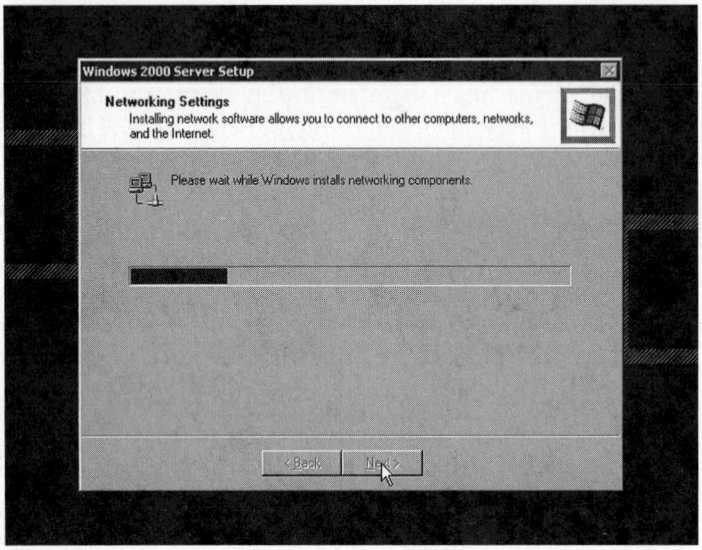

Figure L7-17   Installing networking components

19. In the final step (**Figure L7-18**), Setup (1) Installs the Start Menu, (2) Registers components, (3) Saves settings, and (4) Removes any temporary files used.

20. When your computer reboots again, if there are any hardware devices that were detected for which Windows did not have a correct device driver in its database, you will be prompted to search for the appropriate drivers. At this point the drivers can be anywhere, including the network, if networking was configured for DHCP and there is a DHCP server available.

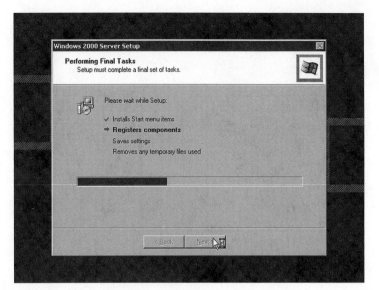

Figure L7-18   Completing the setup

Exercise 2 Review

1. What were the two choices of file system offered during the Disk Preparation sequence?

2. At what point did you have control over your mouse during the installation procedure?

LAB SUMMARY

The previous pages led you through a step-by-step procedure for creating all the necessary floppy disks you may ever need to install WIN2K. You also spend a large portion of your day installing the product. Now you know why network administrators were so happy Microsoft created methods by which large numbers of machines could be configured at once over a network.

LAB

8

CREATING THE SERVER BASELINE

Chapter 14 of the textbook introduces the concept of a server baseline, why you should create one, and what information you need to keep track of in order to make one work. So I won't rehash all that here. You should review that information as you go through the process of creating your own baseline in this lab. Later, you will use this information on a comparative basis when performing upgrades on the system.

EXERCISE 1: CREATING THE BASELINE LOG

The most useful baseline log is the one that is created the first day a server goes on-line. Unfortunately, that's not always possible. However, as a general rule of thumb, any time you bring up a new server, it is wise to create a baseline that runs the whole day. You can be even more thorough and run the monitor for a whole week. If you're going to do that, however, you might want to consider a sample interval somewhat longer than once every minute. Either way, to run a report for an extended period of time, you want to generate a log. To do this in Windows:

1. Click Start>Programs>Administrative Tools>Performance. This will give you the screen you see if **Figure L8-1**.

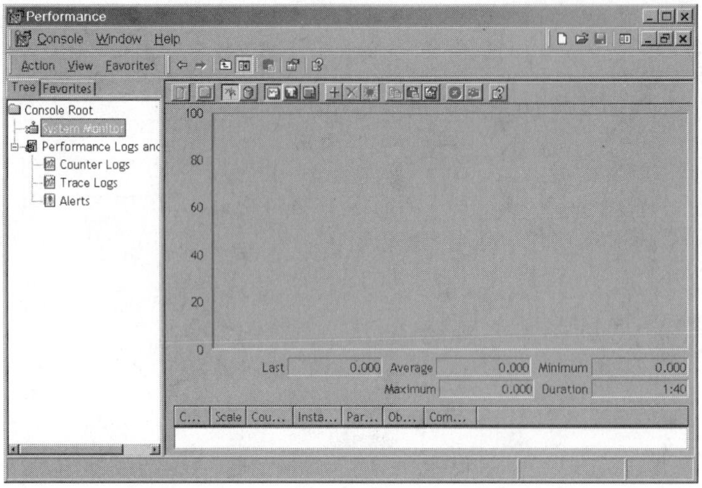

Figure L8-1   Microsoft Performance Monitor

2. Highlight Performance Logs and Alerts

3. In the right-hand pane, right-click Counter Logs.

4. Select New Log Settings, and in the next window (**Figure L8-2**) give those settings a name.

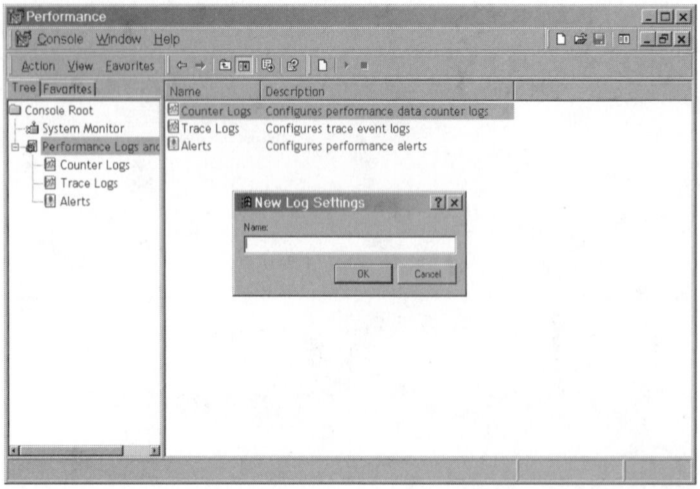

Figure L8-2   It's possible to have more than one collection of settings to monitor. Therefore, it's necessary to create a separate file for each new session you create.

5. Click the Add button in the lower right-hand corner of the Counters box.

6. Select % Processor Time, as shown in **Figure L8-3**, and click Add in the next window. It will appear that nothing happened. It did. Repeat this process for every counter you wish to add.

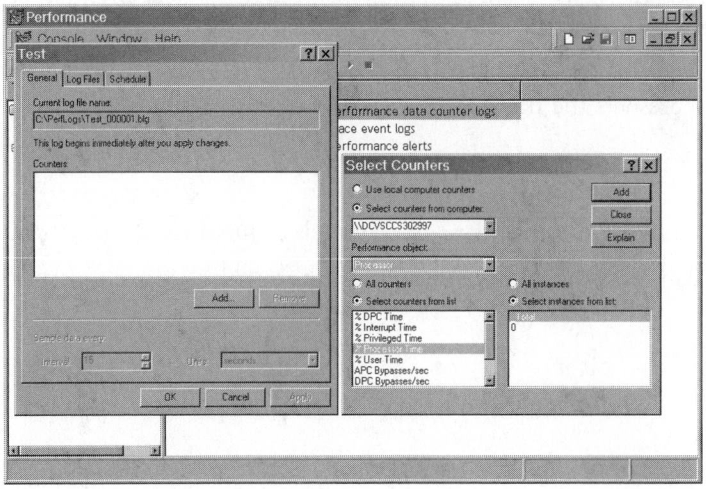

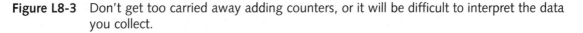

Figure L8-3   Don't get too carried away adding counters, or it will be difficult to interpret the data you collect.

7. When you're finished adding counters, click the Close button.

8. Select an interval. If you plan to monitor all day, select 30 seconds if you don't mind a moderately large, but fairly detailed log. For monitoring an entire week, you might go with once every 2 minutes. In **Figure L8-4**, I have selected one sample for every hour.

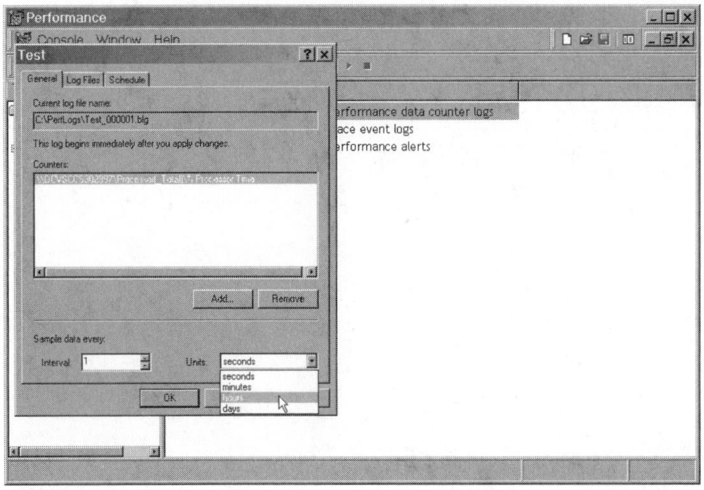

Figure L8.4   The interval you select will determine the size of your final log file. You don't want it to be too small or you won't have a sufficient data set. If it's too large, you'll fall asleep reading it.

9. Click Apply and then OK in your log file window.

10. If this is the first time you've done this, you will get a message warning you that the folder C:\perflogs couldn't be found; do you want to create it? You do if you want to go any further. Click Yes.

11. Now, in the Performance window, right-click your newly created log file and select start. Your baseline data is now being collected.

12. To view a log once it's been created, you can click the System Monitor in the left-hand window of Performance; then, in the right window, click the view log data file icon (orpress Ctrl+L).

13. When you first open your log file, it will seem as though like it didn't collect anything because you can add the counters one at a time as you see fit.

14. Right-click in the right-hand side of the performance screen and select add counters. As you add each one, the graph that represents the data collected for that counter appears.

Exercise 1 Review

1. What are two good counters to watch in order to keep track of memory usage?

2. If you want to show that you need to add a second CPU to the server, what counters should you monitor?

Performing a Memory Upgrade

Sometimes the cure for a sluggish machine is simply to add more memory. As more services are required of the server, or as more users are added to the system, memory requirements increase. If physical memory doesn't increase along with the demand, the paging file gets hit more frequently and, worse yet, data isn't even found there as often. This results in drastically reduced server performance. Adding memory really isn't that big of a deal. But there are some things to watch for to ensure that your project is successful.

EXERCISE 1: BEFORE THE UPGRADE

The preliminary steps for performing a memory upgrade are similar to any other hardware upgrade. You're asking the same questions; however, you have to look in different places to find the answers. The first thing you want to do is to make sure that upgrading the memory is really going to solve your problem. Monitor system performance for several days using the following objects and counters.

     a. Processor Object
        i. % Processor Time
        ii. % User Time
     b. Memory Object
        i. Available Megabytes
        ii. Page Faults/Sec
        iii. Page Writes/Sec

If the data you collect indicates a memory upgrade is in order, then it's time to proceed. Before diving in, perform the following checks.

1. Determine that your system can actually support more memory. Check the documentation that came with the system or, if it is a custom-built system, the motherboard's documentation will help determine this.

2. Ascertain what kind of memory is installed in the system. You will need to make sure that all memory installed in the system is of the same type. A utility such as Everest Home Edition can help you out in that respect. There is a free download available on *http://www.lavalys.com/products/*. Although it is possible that a system might support two or more different types of memory, it won't support both types simultaneously. You must match the new memory with the existing memory.

3. Make sure the capacity of the chip you want to use is supported by your BIOS and chipset. Even though there are 1GB DDR modules available, there are some systems that won't support larger than 512MB modules. Go on-line to the manufacturer's Web site and verify your system's capacity. It's possible that with a BIOS upgrade this limitation can be overcome.

From this point on, the checklist is the same as for other components.

1. Schedule downtime.

2. Notify users.

3. Use proper ESD protection while performing the upgrade.

Exercise 1 Review

1. What are two things you need to check before ordering new memory for your system?

2. If your system currently doesn't support your brand-new 1GB modules, what might you do to make your upgrade happen?

EXERCISE 2: PERFORMING THE UPGRADE

Now for the fun part. We'll dig into the system and add the new memory modules. As always, when digging into the system, take all the necessary precautions to protect the system from static discharge.

1. Power down the system and unplug it from the wall.

2. Ground the computer enclosure to allow static to drain away.

3. Examine the inside of the computer to see what, if any, components need to be removed to gain unrestricted access to the memory slots. Some systems require that nothing be removed; on the other hand, there are systems that require that all the cables be removed and the internal drive bays be taken out.

4. If replacing memory, you'll first need to remove the old module. Follow these steps.

    a. On either side of the base of the memory module are two clips (**Figure L9–1**). Push down firmly on both clips at the same time. This will force the chip up and out of the slot. You'll feel it disengage. Don't be afraid to use a little elbow grease here. On the other hand, if it feels like you're having to add too much pressure, check with your instructor.

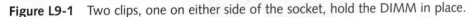

Figure L9-1   Two clips, one on either side of the socket, hold the DIMM in place.

    b. Pull the chip straight up and out.

    c. Place it in the anti-static bag that the new memory module shipped in.

5. To insert the new module, line the slots on the DIMM up to the registration keys in the slot (**Figure L9–2**).

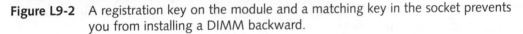

Figure L9-2   A registration key on the module and a matching key in the socket prevents you from installing a DIMM backward.

6. Press firmly down with one thumb on each end of the module until you feel it click into place.

    a. (OPTIONAL STEP) If your system is an older one that uses SIMMs, there will be only one slot on the base of the module. Insert it into the slot by tilting it forward about 45 degrees and snapping it back into place.

7. On the DIMM, snap the two end locks into place if they didn't go all the way in. If there are two modules side-by-side, run the tip of your finger along the top edges of both modules and verify that they are both level. If the new chip is seated at an angle, it means you probably tried to snap it in backward and one of the slots in the base didn't find a registration key. Try again.

8. Replace any components you had to remove and close up the case.

Exercise 2 Review

1. What are two differences between installing SIMMs and DIMMs?

2. What are some components you might need to remove in order to gain access to the memory slots?

EXERCISE 3: AFTER THE UPGRADE IS OVER

You're not done yet. There are still a few menial chores to be done. First, we need to confirm our installation, then we need to document it.

1. Restart the machine and enter the CMOS setup. With many systems, simply restarting the machine will prompt you to do this when POST detects that memory has changed.

2. Verify that the BIOS recognizes the new memory.

   a. If it does, exit the BIOS and watch the POST to see if it records any errors as it counts the new memory (**Figure L9-3**).

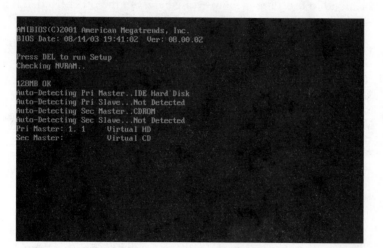

```
AMIBIOS(C)2001 American Megatrends, Inc.
BIOS Date: 08/14/03 19:41:02  Ver: 08.00.02

Press DEL to run Setup
Checking NVRAM..

128MB OK
Auto-Detecting Pri Master..IDE Hard Disk
Auto-Detecting Pri Slave...Not Detected
Auto-Detecting Sec Master..CDROM
Auto-Detecting Sec Slave...Not Detected
Pri Master: 1. 1     Virtual HD
Sec Master:          Virtual CD
```

Figure L9-3   After the installation, POST should recognize the new memory right off the bat.

   b. If it does not, go back into the machine and make sure the memory is properly seated. If the memory is properly seated and you still don't have memory, now is a good time to skip ahead to the diagnostics lab.

3. Let the system boot all the way to the OS.

   a. If you're running Windows, right-click the My Computer icon on the desktop to open the System Properties window. The opening panel shows how much memory the system recognizes on the last line.

   b. On a Linux box, click the Gnome Start button, click Programs>System>System Info. Then click the Detailed Information... box. The middle tab shows memory configuration information.

4. Test the upgrade off the network before adding the system back on.

5. Run a new baseline to verify that the upgrade improved performance

6. Document the upgrade, including a description of the memory modules installed, the vendor who supplied the memory, and the date of purchase.

Exercise 3 Review

1. List two places to check to determine if the system hardware has recognized your upgrade.

2. How do you check total memory in Windows?

3. How do you check total memory in Linux?

EXERCISE 4: MAKING THE MOST OF YOUR MEMORY

Once the new memory has been installed, it might be a good idea to perform some simple steps to optimize memory. There are a couple of things you can do to make the most of what you have.

1. Determine the best settings for a system paging file. Systems are either clients or servers as far as Windows is concerned. By default, when it comes to performance settings, they're all clients. Let's make this one a server.

   a. Right-click My Computer.

b. Click Properties. The System Properties window opens.

c. Click the Advanced tab.

d. Click Performance Options. The screen shown in **Figure L9-4** will appear. On most servers, the Background Services button should be checked. On a desktop machine where the user's applications should take priority, the Applications button should be selected.

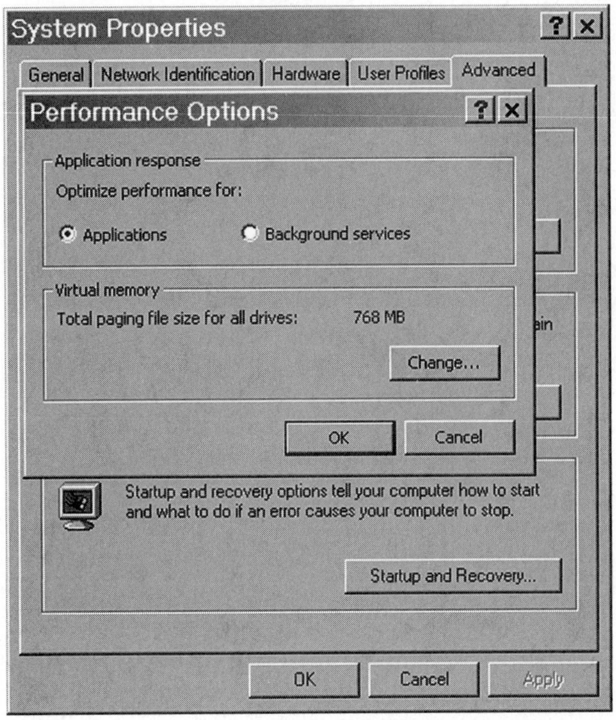

Figure L9-4   The System applet in the Control Panel is where you configure the role of the server.

2. Specifying new paging file settings is the other change you might want to make to your server. If memory is at a premium and you have lots of free hard-disk space, the system defaults for the paging file sizes might not be the best way to go. The paging file has both a minimum and a maximum setting. Windows likes to manage this, but sometimes it is best to take things into your own hands.

a. In that same Performance window, there is a panel labeled Virtual memory. Click the Change button. That will bring up the window in **Figure L9-5**. When Windows was installed, it decided on a minimum and a maximum setting for the paging file based on two factors. One was the amount of memory that was installed and the other was available hard disk space. The more the merrier, I always say (or was that someone else?).

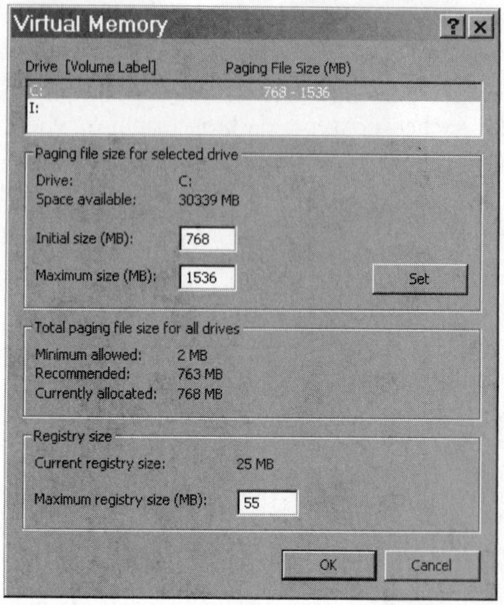

Figure L9-5   The Windows default settings for virtual memory aren't always the best. If you have multiple physical drives, a paging file should exist for each drive.

b. On a system with multiple volumes, you will see more than just Drive C: listed. But by default, only Drive C: will have a paging file configured. Ideally, each volume should have a separate paging file. Change the Initial size (MB): setting to 1024MB and the Maximum size (MB): to 1024MB.

i. So why did we set both sizes to be the same? In the event that the paging file fills up at the minimum setting, there can be a prodigious delay while Windows expands the paging file to the new size. We don't want that to happen, so we're selecting a size that should be suitable. If your system has immense amounts of free hard-disk space, an even larger paging file is not a bad idea.

ii. If you're going to reset the paging file on a system that has been in use for a while, it's a good idea to run Defrag in Safe Mode before resetting the paging file. The paging file cannot be written across fragmented FAUs. It can only be as large as the largest contiguous space available. So even if Windows Explorer says you have 5GB of free space, if the drive is so badly fragmented that only 512MB of contiguous space is available, that's the biggest paging file you can create.

Exercise 4 Review

1. What is the Windows default setting for computer type on any system?

2. Why would you set both the initial and the maximum sizes of the paging file to be the same size?

3. What is the point of running Defrag before reconfiguring a paging file?

10

WORKING WITH ACCOUNTS

In the following exercises, we will be creating several different user and group accounts. These accounts will be used in future labs as we learn to associate permissions and apply security to individual users and groups. We will also learn to copy an account, so that its permissions and settings are automatically applied to the new account that we've created. In the final exercise, we will rename and finally disable our account. In the exercises on groups, I have taken the liberty of using a Windows 2003 Server to show some advanced options. These are optional exercises. If you don't have access to a Windows 2003 Server machine, simply follow along.

CompTIA Objectives Covered in This Lab

Unfortunately, account setup is not in the CompTIA exam. It is, however, information critical to anyone working with computers on a professional level.

Exercise 1: Creating a New Account

Any time a new user is added to the network, that person will require a unique user account. This account, complete with user ID and password, is their ticket to the network. In order to create the account we will perform the following procedures.

1. Click on Start>Programs>Administrative Tools>Active Directory Users and Computers (as seen in **Figure L10-1**).

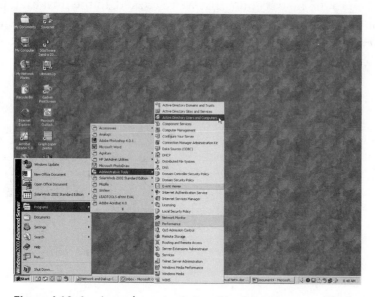

Figure L10-1   A roadmap to Active Directory Users and Computers

2. You should get a screen similar to that in **Figure L10-2**. Highlight Users in the left pane, then in the right pane, right-click in any blank area. From the pop-up menu that appears, select New>User.

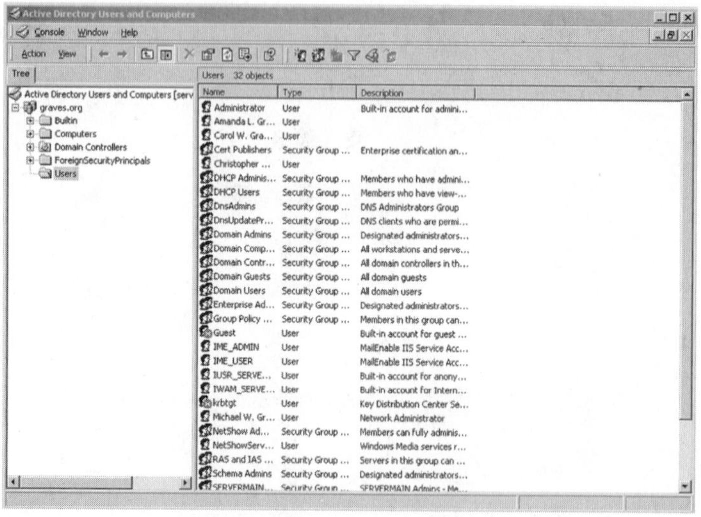

Figure L10-2   The Active Directory Users and Computers console

3. You should now have the screen shown in **Figure L10-3**. Type in the user information as requested. In the User Logon Name: field, type in the User ID for that user. This must be a unique value. There can be no duplicate User IDs anywhere on the network. Click Next.

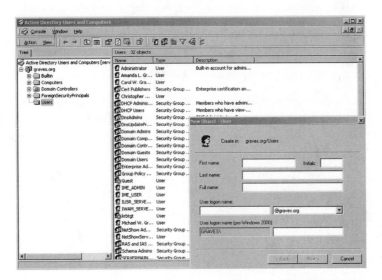

Figure L10-3   Fill in the user information and provide a unique User ID

4. In the next screen (illustrated in **Figure L10-4**), you will be prompted to enter the user's password. You must enter it a second time to confirm the password. Should you inadvertently enter it differently the second time, the password will be rejected and you will have to start again. There are four checkboxes beneath the password fields for password options. These options are as follows:

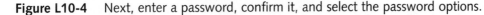

Figure L10-4   Next, enter a password, confirm it, and select the password options.

   a. User must change password at next logon: If this choice is selected, the first time the user logs on to their new account, they will be told that their password has expired and will be prompted to enter a new one (twice, for confirmation). This is the option to select if you want your users selecting their own passwords.

   b. User cannot change password: As the phrase implies, once you have assigned a password, it is etched in stone. Only an account administrator or one with administrative privileges can change the password.

    c. Password never expires: If this field is selected, the password will remain valid until changed by an account administrator or someone with administrative privileges. This is the case even if the password policy has been set to force users to change their password periodically.

    d. Account is disabled: This option prevents anyone from logging on to the network using that particular account. It does not, however, delete any security settings or permissions.

5. For all accounts in our lab exercises, we will be using *password* as our standard password. This will prevent forgotten passwords. Obviously, in a real-world scenario, this would be a very bad idea. Select User cannot change password and click Next.

6. You will get a summary screen like the one in **Figure L10-5**. All the information you typed in will be displayed except for the password. Click Finish. Your new account has been established. Next, enter a password, confirm it, and select the password options.

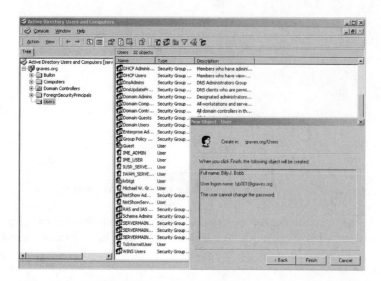

Figure L10-5   The User Summary Screen

7. Repeat the above steps until you have created a total of twelve new accounts. Don't forget to use *password* as the password for all user accounts.

Exercise 1 Review

1. Where do you go to create a new user account in WINXP?

2. What happens if you don't configure a password for XP?

EXERCISE 2: CREATING GROUP ACCOUNTS

Every network administrator quickly learns that managing groups of accounts all at once is much simpler than trying to manage the users one at a time. In this section, we will create two forms of group accounts. We will create local groups to manage resources and we will create global groups to manage users. Later on we'll use these global groups to manage permissions.

Managing Groups

When you are first getting started with networking, it sometimes gets confusing as to when to use groups and when not to. When it comes to managing groups, what is the difference between *global group* and *local group*?

It isn't really all that complicated. Local groups are used to manage local resources. We might have a database containing our customer information. In order to allow access to that database, we create a local group called DATA. Permissions are assigned at this level.

Global groups are used to provide users with similar sets of responsibilities and resource needs the permissions they need to do their work. For example, we might have a global group called SALES. Every salesperson needs access to the same resources and generally needs the same permission sets. Therefore, when we hire a new salesperson, rather than assigning those permissions independently (and remembering what they are), you simply create a new account and add it to the SALES group. In order to give all sales reps access to the database, we add the global group SALES to the local group DATA. In one step, all sales reps were give exactly the same permissions to use the database.

A simple little pneumonic will help you remember these groups. AGLP. *A*ccounts go into *G*lobal groups, which are added to *L*ocal groups, which are given *P*ermissions.

10

Exercise 2a: Creating a Local Group

1. Start Active Directory Users and Computers, just as we did in Exercise 1. Right-click on a blank portion of the right pane and select New>Group from the pop-up menu. You'll get the screen shown in **Figure L10-6**.

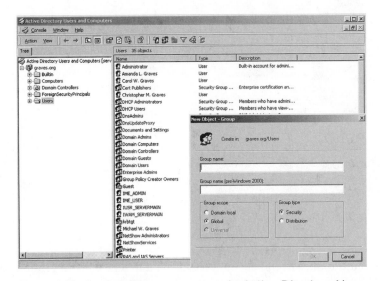

Figure L10-6   Creating a new group in Active Directory Users and Computers

2. For Group Name, type in Documents. Notice that it fills in the field labeled Group Name (pre-Windows 2000) for you. Beneath those fields, on the left are the options D̲omain local and G̲lobal. Select D̲omain local. For now, don't worry about group type. Click OK.

3. Repeat the process, creating a group called DATA.

Exercise 2b: Creating a Global Group

1. Repeat the steps outlined in Exercise 2a. Name the group SALES. The difference is that, instead of selecting Domain local in the second screen, we will select Global.

2. Repeat this process twice, creating global groups called MANAGEMENT and ADMINISTRATION.

Exercise 2 Review

1. What is the difference between a local group and a global group?

2. What is the advantage to using groups?

EXERCISE 3: COPYING AN ACCOUNT

Now that we have created all those nearly identical groups and accounts the hard way, we'll learn how we can take an account that has been configured the way we want and make a new one using the first one as a template.

1. The first thing we want to do is customize an account so that we know it is different from the others we created. Select one of your accounts that you created in Exercise 1 and double-click on it in the right pane of Active Directory Users and Computers. You'll get the screen shown in **Figure L10-7**.

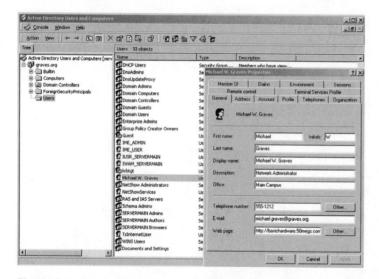

Figure L10-7   Customizing an account

2. Click the tab labeled Member Of. Then click Add. This will give you the screen seen in **Figure L10-8**. As shown in the illustration, add this account to several different built-in groups. Also, add it to your newly created SALES group. Click OK.

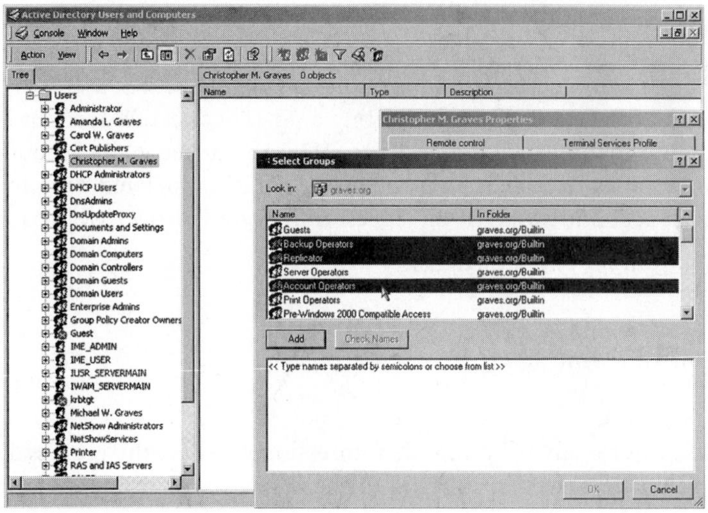

Figure L10-8   Making an account a member of a group

3. Open the Users Folder in the left pane of Active Directory Users and Computers and right-click on the account you just modified. Select Copy. The screens that follow are the same ones you saw when creating a new account because you are essentially creating a new account. Except this new account brings with it all the components of the account you copied.

Exercise 3 Review

1. Why would you want to copy an account as opposed to simply creating one from scratch?

EXERCISE 4: RENAMING AN ACCOUNT

Occasionally, it becomes necessary to rename an account. It's tempting to simply delete the old account and create a new one. However, there is a problem inherent in that procedure. It is not the user name, user ID or password – or any combination – that identifies the account to the OS. The account is identified by a 32-bit number that was generated by the OS when the account was created. This is the account's *security ID* (SID). If you want to keep the entire history of the account intact, you need to keep the SID intact. You do this by renaming the existing account. Here is how to do it.

1. Open Active Directory Users and Computers and open the Users folder.

2. Right-click on the account you want changed.

3. From the pop-up menu, select Rename.

4. Type in the new name for the account.

It's as simple as that.

Exercise 4 Review

1. What is the disadvantage of deleting the account of a user when they leave the company?

2. What is the purpose of the SID?

EXERCISE 5: DISABLING AN ACCOUNT

When a user leaves an organization, the first thing many administrators do is to delete that user's account. This can be (and frequently is) a critical error. The reason for not deleting a no-longer active account is the same one I gave for not creating a new account for an existing user. That SID is the ticket to the account's history. Should you need to access that account for any reason, it won't be possible if it was deleted. Simply recreating it won't work. Fortunately, disabling an account is one of the easiest things you'll ever have to do.

1. Open Active Directory Users and Computers.
2. Open the Users folder.
3. Right-click on the account you want disabled.
4. Select Disable.

Should you need to reactivate that account for any reason in the future, simply repeat the process. Except this time, the option Enable has replaced Disable. Select Enable and the account is now reactivated.

11

CONFIGURING DHCP

CompTIA Objectives Covered in This Lab

1.3 Know the basic purpose and function of the following types of servers (DHCP).

2.3 Develop the server management plan

In my opinion, the Dynamic Host Configuration Protocol (DHCP) beats the heck out of sliced bread, as far as innovation is concerned. With a properly configured DHCP server, I don't have to walk around the entire site changing each computer just because the IP address of a DNS server changed. If I want to force a configuration change onto the users, I simply add it to the DCHP options. Of course, for all this to work, you need to correctly configure DHCP to begin with. In this lab, you will do two things. First, you'll set up your server to become a DHCP server. In the second part, you'll see how to configure the different DHCP options.

EXERCISE 1: CONFIGURING DHCP

Installing DCHP isn't particularly difficult, nor is it confusing. That's why it baffles me every time I see a network that still uses static IP configuration. In this exercise, you will configure your servers to act as DHCP servers.

The first thing you need to do is plan your configuration. What is the range of available IP addresses? What devices on the network are you using that *require* static IPs, things such as router interfaces, server interfaces, and printers? You must prevent DHCP from doling these addresses out. Lastly, are there any pieces of network information that might be more easily changed with DHCP? This last question is one we will examine in Exercise 2: Configuring Options.

For the purposes of this exercise, you will configure your DHCP scope to cover the range of 192.168.2.10 to 192.168.2.110. You want to reserve a large number of IP addresses for static configuration, so you are going to exclude two ranges: 192.168.2.30 to 50 and 192.168.2.75 to 90. Let's get started.

1. Open Control Panel and double-click Administrative Tools. One of the icons you'll see is one for DHCP (**Figure L11-1**).

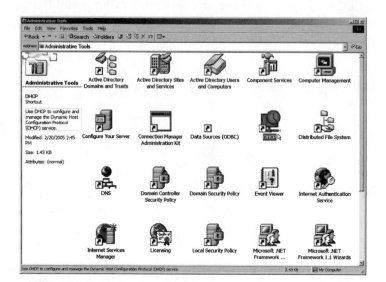

Figure L11-1 DHCP management is one of the Administrative Tools you'll find in Control Panel.

2. Highlight the server name you want to configure. On a larger network, you might see several machines listed here. Unless your classroom is networked and you're all sharing a network address, you should only see your own machine at this point in time. (**See Figure L11-2**.)

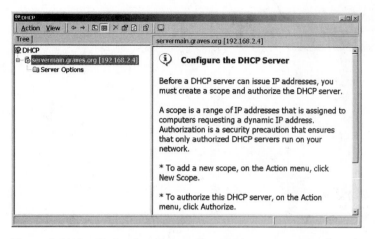

Figure L11-2   To begin your configuration, you must select the server you wish to manage.

3. For DHCP to work, you must give it a range of addresses that it can dole out. This range of addresses is called the *scope*. To configure a new scope, click on <u>A</u>ction and then select New Scope, as seen in **Figure L11-3**.

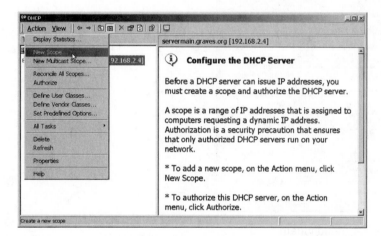

Figure L11-3   For DHCP to work, you need to configure a scope of addresses.

4. The applet that creates a new DHCP scope is called the New Scope Wizard. You are probably looking at it on your screen right now, but if you are simply following along with the illustrations, it looks like **Figure L11-4**. Click <u>N</u>ext.

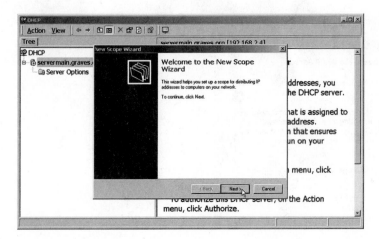

Figure L11-4   As with everything else Microsoft does, creating a scope is accomplished
with a Wizard.

5. It's possible for one DHCP server to host multiple scopes. Therefore, it is necessary for each one to have a unique name (**Figure L11-5**). Name the scope and give it a description. Click **N**ext.

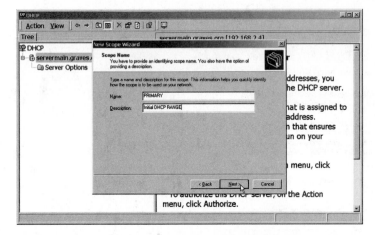

Figure L11-5   Give your new scope a friendly name.

6. The idea of a scope is that it contains a wide range of different addresses. Type in the beginning and ending IP addresses of your range, as seen in **Figure L11-6**. Subnet masks will fill in automatically. Don't worry about the fact that you want to statically assign some of these addresses. We'll "address" that issue later.

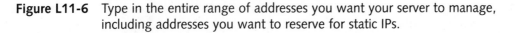

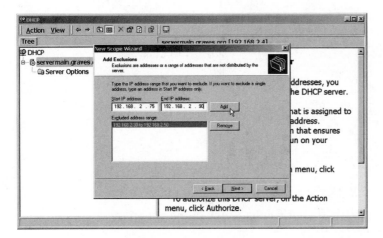

Figure L11-6   Type in the entire range of addresses you want your server to manage, including addresses you want to reserve for static IPs.

7. Type in your exclusions. Remember that you are adding two sets. The first set of exclusions runs from 192.168.2.30 to 50 and the second runs from 192.168.2.75 to 90. After your exclusions range is in (**Figure L11-7**), click A<u>d</u>d. Add a second range if you so desire. I did. When you're finished, click <u>N</u>ext.

Figure L11-7   Here is where you tell DHCP what addresses you want to reserve for static IP assignments.

8. IP addresses handed out by DHCP aren't permanent assignments. You can control how long a user can hang onto a given address with a lease (**Figure L11-8**). If you're managing Internet service accounts, you want a very low lease, such as 1 minute. As long as the user is connected, they get to keep their address. For a conventional network, a good value is 7 days. Click <u>N</u>ext.

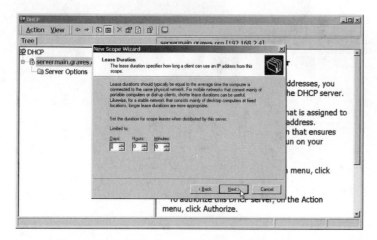

Figure L11-8 The address lease dictates how long a user retains an address before DHCP reconfigures the user's NIC.

9. Now you have the option of configuring the DHCP options (**Figure L11-9**). Because I want to go over adding these after the fact, click N<u>o</u>. I will configure these options later. Click <u>N</u>ext.

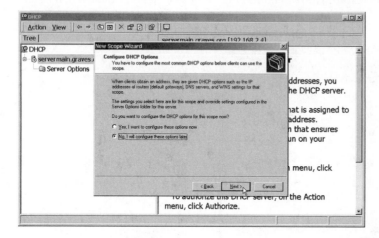

Figure L11-9 For the purposes of this lab, do not configure any of the options here. We'll do it later.

10. At this point in time, you have almost finished your DHCP configuration. There's just one more little step. In the Completing DHCP Wizard screen (**Figure L11-10**) that follows, click Finish.

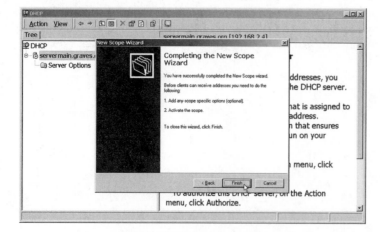

Figure L11-10 Completing DHCP isn't *quite* completing the configuration.

11. In the DHCP management console, you now have your scope shown. If you click on the + sign next to the scope, it will open to show all the options as seen in **Figure L11-11**.

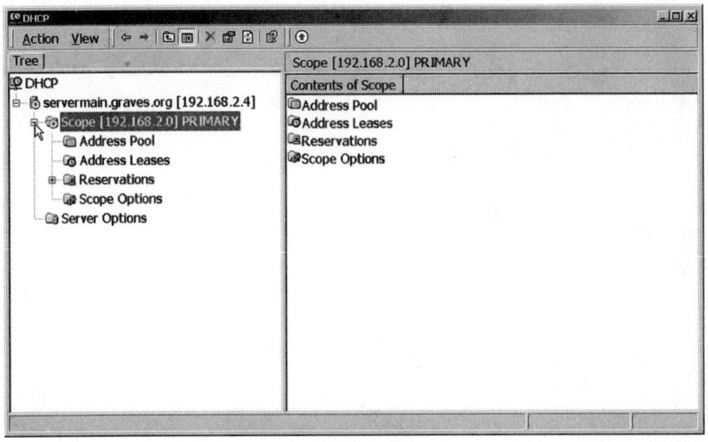

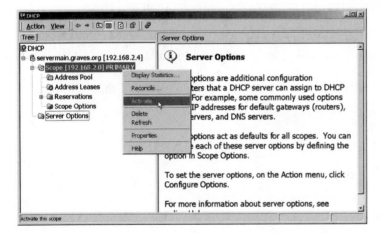

Figure L11-11   Once you've finished the Wizard, your new scope will appear in the DCHP management console.

12. You're still not done yet. Until the scope is activated, it is useless. Right–click the scope name and in the menu that pops up, click Activate (as seen in **Figure L11-12**). *Now* you're finished.

Figure L11-12   Before your new scope actually works, you must activate it. Was this a preview of things to come with Microsoft?

Exercise 1 Review

1. What are the two things you need to configure in DHCP to make your server into a DHCP server?

2. What is the term for the addresses you want to prevent DHCP from handing out over the network?

3. What is the last thing you must do before your DHCP server is really a DHCP server?

EXERCISE 2: CONFIGURING OPTIONS

In the first exercise, we skipped configuring the DHCP options so you could do it separately. We will configure the DHCP options in the following section.

1. Highlight Scope Options in the DHCP window. Click Action>Configure Options, as seen in **Figure L11–13**. There are literally dozens of options available to configure. In this lab, you'll configure a DNS server and a router in your options.

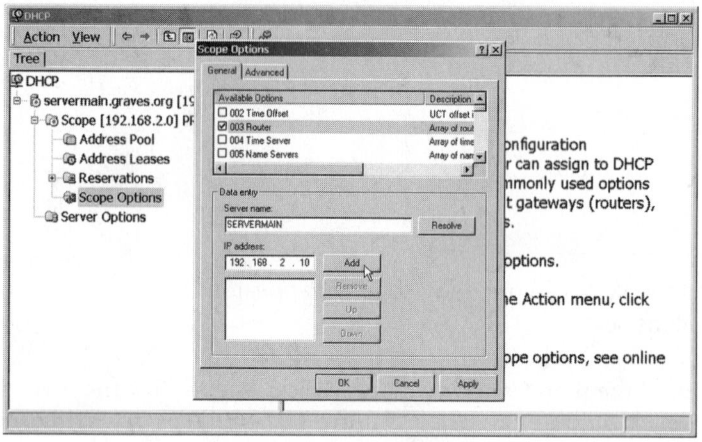

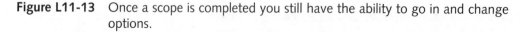

Figure L11-13   Once a scope is completed you still have the ability to go in and change options.

2. Click the Router box, and options for a server name and IP address appear. In a real installation, you would need to know the actual information for your router. For this exercise, simply type in your own computer's NetBIOS name and IP address. Click Add and then OK.

3. Repeat the same process for the DNS server. Whew! That was rough, wasn't it?

Exercise 2 Review

1. What is the process for configuring the options in DHCP?

2. What are the two pieces of information you need to tell DHCP for it to configure client computers for DNS?

12

CONFIGURING A DNS SERVER

These days it is almost impossible to stumble across a network that isn't connected to the Internet. Even so-called secure networks rely on Internet connections for e-mail services at the very least. For those networks that require browsing services, it might be a good idea to configure a server that provides Domain Name System (DNS) services. Although it is definitely possible to rely on the DNS servers of your ISP, browser speed can be improved by hosting your own server. In this lab, we're going to install and configure DNS services. To complete the lab you're going to need:

- The student machine for each student, booted to Windows Server

- The installation CD for Windows Server

Estimated time for this lab is approximately 30 minutes.

EXERCISE 1: INSTALLING DNS SERVER

Because we did not let the Autoconfigure Wizard run, the first thing you need to do is install DNS server. That's easy enough. We'll let a wizard do that part for us. Before you begin, make sure that your machine is assigned a static IP address. DNS won't run on a server configured to get its IP address via DHCP. Start by opening the Windows Components Wizard.

1. Click Start>Control Panel>Add or Remove Programs.

2. Click Add/Remove Windows Components. That'll bring up the screen shown in **Figure L12-1**.

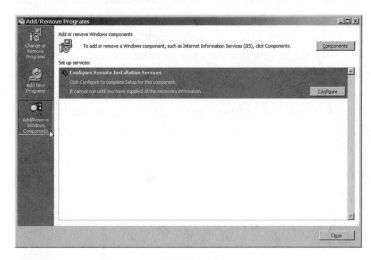

Figure L12-1   Add/Remove Programs

3. Click the Components button and in the screen that appears select the Networking Services check box as seen in **Figure L12-2**, and then click Details.

Figure L12-2   Adding Windows Components

4. In Subcomponents of Networking Services, which is the next window to pop up (**Figure L12-3**), select the Domain Name System (DNS) check box, click OK, and then click Next.

5. If you are prompted, in Copy files from, type the full path of the distribution files, and then click OK. Restart your machine.

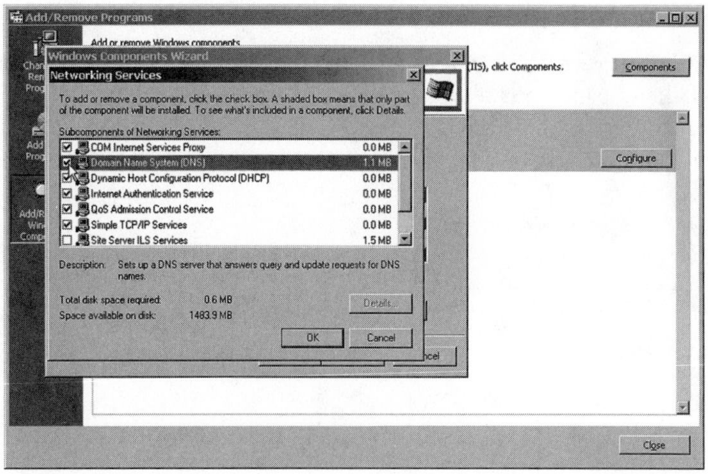

Figure L12-3 Select DNS.

Exercise 1 Review

1. Where did you have to go to install the Subcomponents of Networking Services?

2. What type of IP address does the DNS server need to have?

EXERCISE 2: CONFIGURING DNS

Now it's time to configure DNS. It's one thing to blithely follow along filling in the blanks as you're told. It's another thing to understand what it is you're doing. When configuring DNS, you are going to create a *forward lookup zone* and *a reverse lookup zone*. A forward lookup zone is simply a process by which your server uses a host name provided by the user to resolve an IP address. It does so in one of two ways. The whole time your server is on-line, it dynamically maintains tables of every host it looks up. It also has in its tables the IP addresses of all the *dot servers*. (For a complete discussion on DNS, refer to *The Complete Guide to Networking and Network+*, by this author). When presented with a new query, the server first checks its own tables to see if it already knows the address. If that fails, it queries the appropriate dot server.

A reverse lookup zone allows a DNS server to perform the opposite trick. It takes an IP address and uses it to look up a host name. A DNS server will function without a reverse lookup zone. However, it isn't difficult to configure and you need one if your server is to have full DNS functionality.

You also need to select the type of lookup zone you are creating. When selecting a DNS zone type, there are three choices:

- Active Directory (AD) Integrated
- Standard Primary
- Standard Secondary

AD Integrated uses the Lightweight Directory Access Protocol (LDAP). This option will appear only if AD is configured. If it is configured and you select this option, AD will store and replicate your zone files.

In a Standard Primary zone, DNS database entries are stored as simple text files. It is a primary zone because your server is creating and maintaining the database. This text file can be shared with other DNS servers that store their information in a text file. A Standard Secondary zone copies its information from another DNS server.

To configure our DNS server, we're not going to use a wizard. We're going to do it the old-fashioned way.

1. Click Start>Programs>Administrative Tools>DNS to launch the DNS console seen in **Figure L12-4**. You'll see in the left-hand pane your server listed by its NetBIOS name. Click on the name to highlight your server, and in the right-hand pane two entries for Forward Lookup Zone and Reverse Lookup Zone will appear.

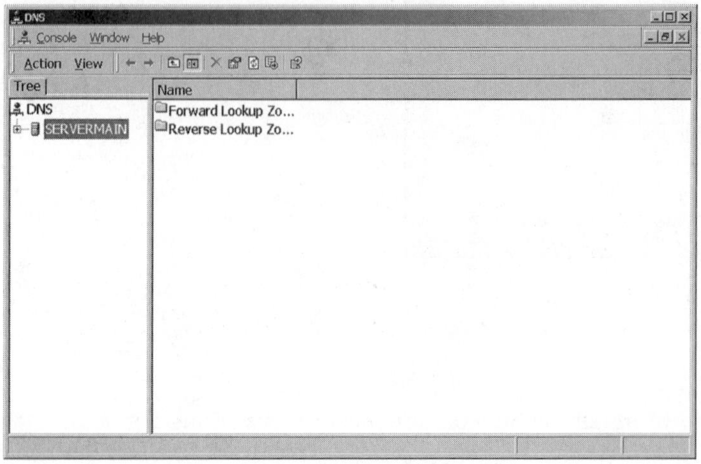

Figure L12-4   The DNS management console

2. Click <u>A</u>ction>New Zone. A screen will pop up prompting you to select the type of zone you are creating (**Figure L12-5**). Select Standard primary.

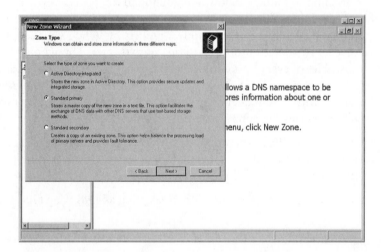

Figure L12-5   First, you select the type of zone you're configuring.

3. Now you need to name your zone (**Figure L12-6**). Each zone on the server must have a unique name. Give your lookup zone a name.

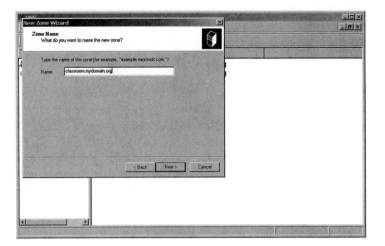

Figure L12-6   Then you give your zone a name.

Exercise 2 Review

1. What is the role of the forward lookup zone?

2. How does a forward lookup zone differ from a reverse lookup zone?

12

13

THE EVENT VIEWER

Objectives of Network+ Exam Covered in this Lab

3.1 Identify the basic capabilities (i.e., client support, interoperability, authentication, file and print services, application support, and security) of the following server operating systems: Windows.

4.7 Given output from a diagnostic utility (e.g., tracert, ping, ipconfig, etc.), identify the utility and interpret the output.

4.11 Given a network troubleshooting scenario involving a client connectivity problem (e.g., incorrect protocol/client software/authentication configuration, or insufficient rights/ permission), identify the cause of the problem.

One of the better troubleshooting tools provided by W2KS is one called *Event Viewer*. Event viewer collects information on different activities that are generated by either hardware or software action. These events range from benign to critical, and Event Viewer frequently can provide information that helps the administrator diagnose what lead up to the event.

Event Viewer reports three degrees of severity in its logs. These degrees of severity are described in Table 13-1.

Table 13-1 Event Viewer Severity Classifications

Symbol	Severity	Description
	Information	Describes the successful operation of an application, driver, or service.
	Error	A significant problem, such as loss of data or loss of functionality.
	Warning	An event that is not necessarily significant, but may indicate a possible future problem.

With this information in mind, let's look at our Event Viewer and see what we can find.

EXERCISE 1: AN OVERVIEW OF EVENT VIEWER

1. Click on Start>Programs>Administrative Tools>Event Viewer. The Screen in **Figure L13-1** will appear. Here, I added a computer that had not been on my network since rebuilding the domain. That gives us some interesting errors to examine.

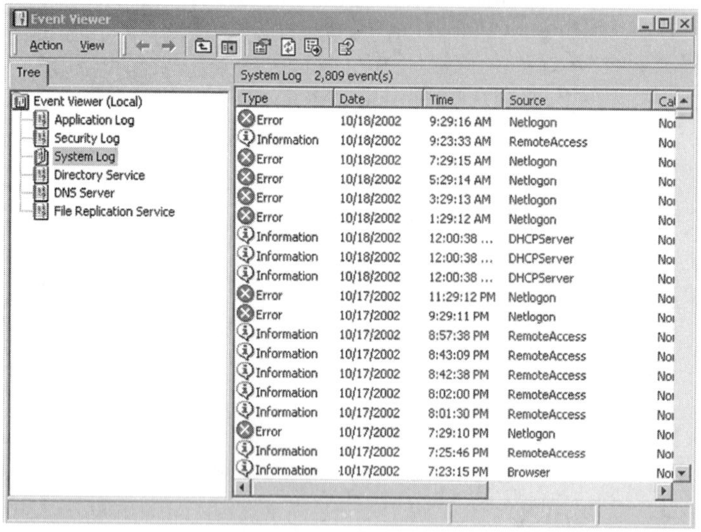

Figure L13-1 The Event Viewer Screen

2. Notice that in the left-hand pane there are six different aspects of system performance that are logged. These are:

   a. Application Log: Events logged by applications or programs are recorded here.

   b. Security Log: Events such as invalid logon attempts are recorded here. If you have auditing enabled, this is where auditing events will be stored.

   c. System Log: Any event generated by a system component, whether it is hardware (such as a memory error) or OS related, will be stored here.

   d. Directory Service Log: Events directly related to Active Directory are recorded here.

   e. DNS Server: Events generated by DNS services are stored here.

   f. File Replication Service: Events generated by the File Replication service are stored here. An example of this event would be the failure of two domain controllers to successfully replicate the SID or SYSVOL.

3. Highlight the Application Log in the left-hand pane. Click Action. Click Properties. This will bring up the screen in **Figure L13-2**. The two tabs in this screen are General and Filter. Under General, you can configure several different elements.

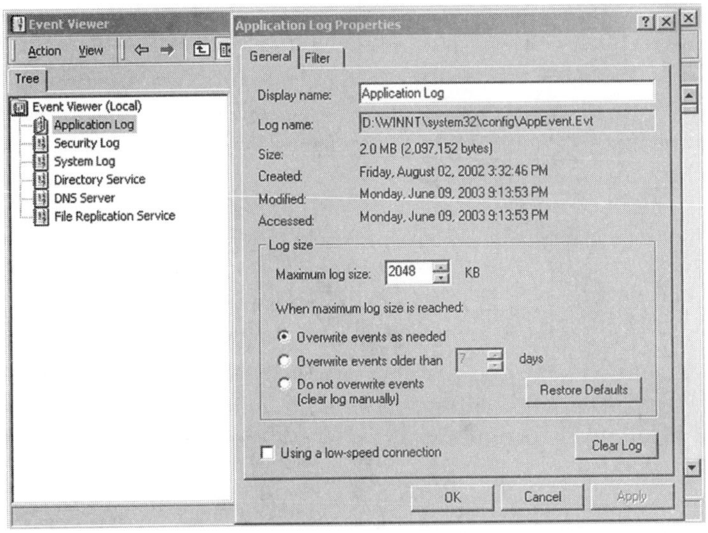

Figure L13-2   Application Log properties.

4. Under Display Name, change Application Log to Server Applications. Click Apply and then OK. Notice the change on your Event Viewer Screen.

5. Go back to the Properties screen for the Application Log and change it back to its original name. Notice that the default Maximum log size is 512KB. Also, by default, when the log size exceeds 512KB, it is set to Overwrite events older than 7 days. If hard drive space is not an issue, I suggest that your log should be increased to 2,048KB (2MB) and that the selection Overwrite events as needed be selected. Make these changes

6. Another option on this screen is to Clear log. Clicking on this button will completely delete all events recorded in this log. You will be asked if you want to save the log files before you continue (**Figure L13-3**). We don't really want to clear our log, so click Cancel and let's move on.

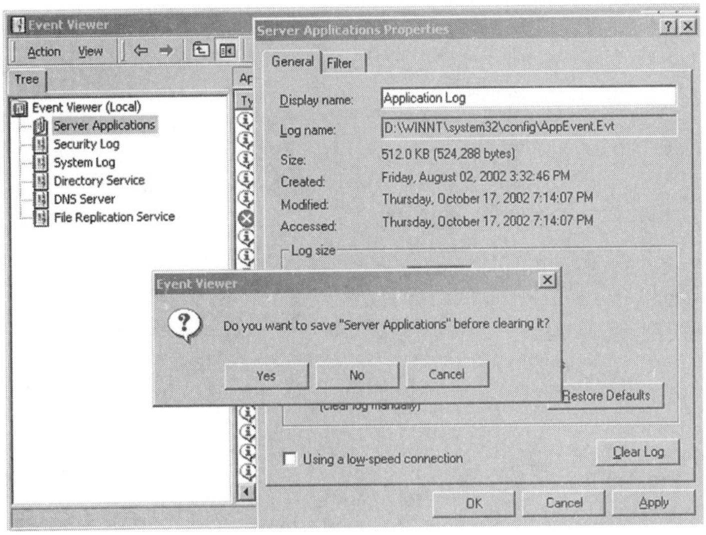

Figure L13-3   Think twice before you clear the log. You can't get it back.

Exercise 1 Review

1. Where would we find the Event View in Windows 2000?

2. If a service fails to start, what kind of icon will it display?

3. You have configured your server to audit failed logon attempts. Where are reports of these events logged?

EXERCISE 2: ANALYZING AN EVENT

1. For this exercise, go to the System Log. This is where you will find the most events. Because it is impossible for me to predict what all of your systems will look like, follow closely with the illustrations in addition to performing these steps on your computer. My descriptions of events and other information will be based entirely on the illustrations.

2. Double-click on any error your System Log may be reporting. If there are no errors, find an Information event. Lacking that, double-click on any event, but follow the text carefully. Double-clicking on any event will bring up the Event Properties screen (**Figure L13-4**).

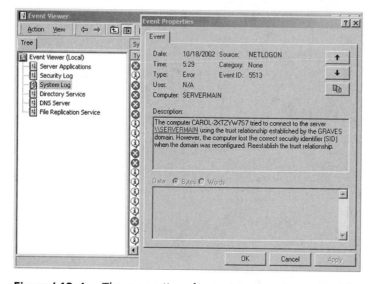

Figure L13-4 The properties of any given event can provide some good troubleshooting tips.

3. If you are looking at an error message, such as the one in the illustration, the description screen will tell you precisely what failed. In the case of the error in the illustration, you are even told how to fix the problem. All you need to do is rejoin this computer to the domain. (See Lab Seven for details on adding a computer account to the domain.)

4. Close Event Viewer.

Troubleshooting the NOS through Events

Beginning network administrators are often overwhelmed at first. This feeling will pass and you will find that all providers of network operating systems offer a substantial amount of support for their product. In Windows 2000 and XP, the Event Viewer provides information on what caused a failure. If this doesn't help, you may use their TechNet services on their Web page (currently at *http://www.microsoft.com/technet/*). A search of key words from the message will likely bring up several articles related to your problem. Novell offers similar services and Linux help can be obtained from Red Hat, Mandrake, and numerous other Linux vendors.

Another good resource for Microsoft users is the Windows 2000 or Windows XP Resource Guide. Again, Novell provides similar references for its NOS. In this kit, you will find reams of information. Nearly every error message generated by the NOS is explained and most causes of service or driver failure can be found in this guide. These are expensive books, but compared to the cost of your NOS and/or the cost of the administrator's time, the resource guide is an essential tool for any administrator.

Exercise 2 Review

1. What kinds of information can we learn from an event if we double-click on it?

2. If a service fails to start, what can we learn by examining the event?

13

14

AN OVERVIEW OF THE REGISTRY EDITOR

The Control Panel is a safe place for making changes to the registry for common issues. However, occasionally, something comes up in Windows that requires that the Registry be surgically edited. Should this need arise, *be careful!* With some of the Registry settings, simply having a single character missing or out of place can render your system unstable or even unbootable. Fortunately, Windows users have access to a utility that allows them to back off to a previous version of the Registry. This utility varies from version to version. As with Lab Seven, all you need to complete this lab is the Student Computer equipped with KB, monitor, and Mouse. Once again, there are no specific Core Exam objectives covered here. This is simply information you need to survive.

EXERCISE 1: AN OVERVIEW OF THE REGISTRY EDITOR

1. The Registry Editor is one of those utilities that Microsoft has deliberately concealed from the average user. There are no icons to click on; instead it is a command line utility. It can be run either from a DOS window or from the Start>Run command line. In Windows 98, this utility is launched by typing the command regedit at either the command prompt or from the Start>Run command line. Windows 2000 and 2003 Server users may choose from two different versions of this utility. Typing regedit gets basically the same utility that Windows 98 users have. A safer, but perhaps less potent version comes from typing regedt32 at the prompt. The latter does not have quite as powerful a search function, but it does allow the user to set security settings on individual registry keys within the editor. Because regedit is available to both, we will describe it here.

2. Click Start>Run and type regedit in the command line. You will get the window seen in **Figure L14-1**. The left-hand window of the screen is known as the *navigation area,* and the right-hand window is the *topic area.*

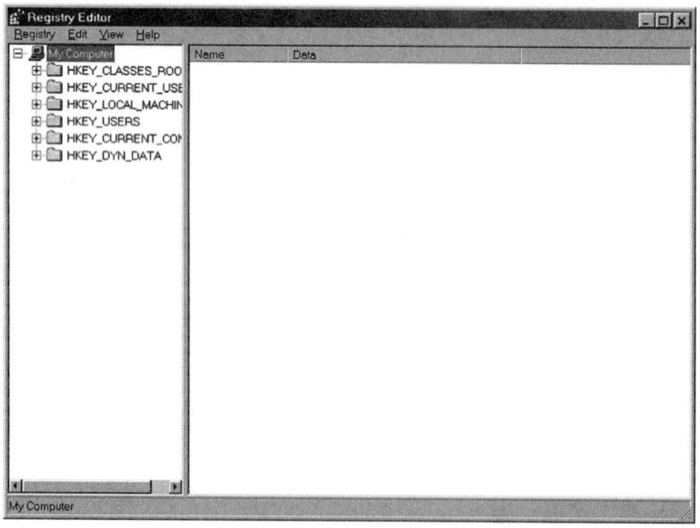

Figure L14-1   The opening screen to the registry editor

3. The Windows registry has six different *keys* that are stored collectively in two different files. The files are user.dat and system.dat. A third file is created optionally when System Policies are enabled. This file is called config.pol. The keys are:

    a. HKEY_CLASSES_ROOT: This key contains the information needed for linking objects between different applications, determining what file types are opened by what applications and for mapping a specific function to keystroke patterns or mouse clicks.

    b. HKEY_CURRENT_USER: This is where user-specific information is stored, including the programs in the user's start menu, desktop settings, applications that appear on the desktop, and display preferences.

    c. HKEY_LOCAL_MACHINE: Information specific to the computer, including device drivers, installed software, and installed hardware, can be found in this key.

    d. HKEY_USERS: Windows supports the ability to allow several different users to log onto the same machine, and if so desired, each user can have their own specific settings and preferences. This key stores the preferences and settings for all users.

    e. HKEY_CURRENT_CONFIG: As we saw in Lab Seven, it is possible to set up multiple hardware profiles on the same computer. Whereas HKEY_LOCAL_MACHINE stores all hardware and software information, HKEY_CURRENT_CONFIG loads the information specific to the profile chosen during boot.

f. HKEY_DYN_DATA: This key stores dynamically configured information concerning the status of Plug 'n Play at the time of boot. Changes to device settings that do not require a reboot are are managed by this key. This key is created by Windows at each startup and is not stored in any permanent file.

4. Beneath each of these primary keys are collections of *hives*. Hives are sub-keys that contain information specific to a particular aspect of the machine. Click on the + next HKEY_LOCAL_MACHINE in the navigation area to open up the hive. You should get a screen similar to **Figure L14–2**.

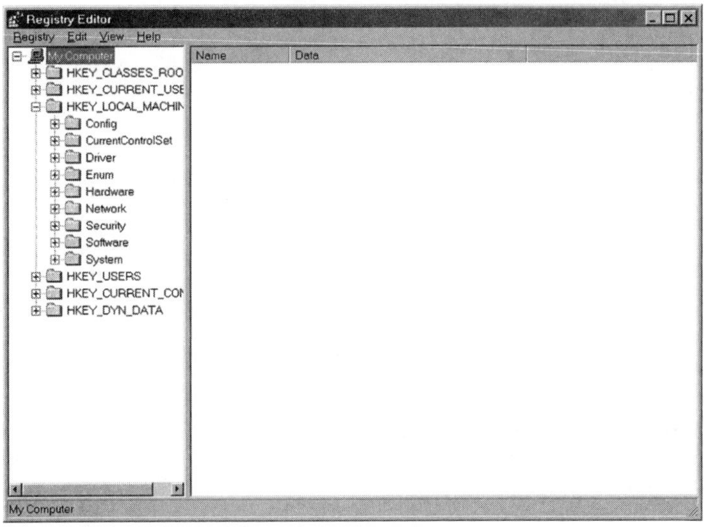

Figure L14-2   The Hives of HKEY_LOCAL_MACHINE

5. If all you did was click on the + sign, as instructed, there is still nothing in the topic area. Open the Software hive, then the Microsoft folder and scroll all the way down to Windows. Open the Windows folder and highlight CurrentVersion. You should get a screen similar to that seen in **Figure L14–3**.

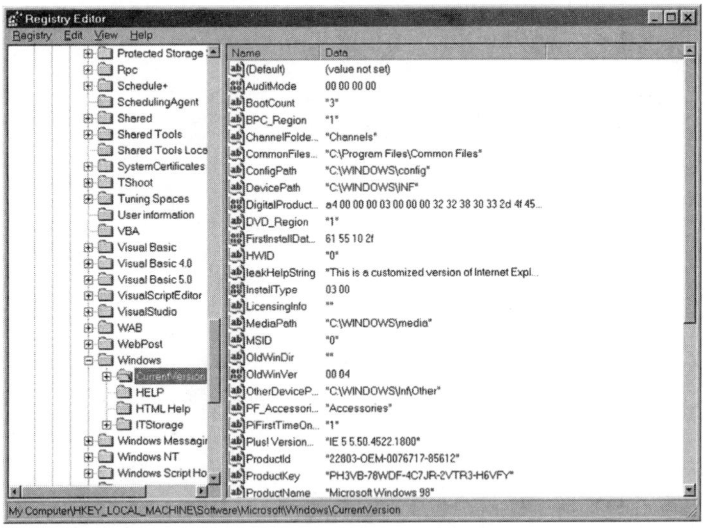

Figure L14-3   The assorted values of CurrentVersion

6. To see the type of data that is stored in a particular entry, double-click on FirstInstallDateTime. Hmmm, they seem to have encrypted this. Wonder why they might have done that?

14

7. Now, so far, you haven't changed anything in the registry (or at least I hope you haven't). Before we do anything that drastic, we want to have a backup of the registry. To do that, highlight My Computer at the very top of the navigation area. Then click Registry>Export Registry File. The default location to save the file is in the My Documents folder. Accept the default folder and name your backup regbackup.reg. Now if you screw anything up beyond recognition, you can restore your system.

Exercise 1 Review

1. What are the two primary files that contain the Registry?

2. What additional file is created if you choose to enable system policies?

3. List the six primary keys of the Registry.

4. Where would settings specific to hardware installed on the system be stored?

5. Where would you look for the settings that dictate how a particular file behaves if double-clicked?

EXERCISE 2: EDITING THE REGISTRY

If you haven't made your registry backup yet, *do not continue.* Go back to the last step in Exercise 1 and complete it before proceeding.

1. We want to make a change that is benign and won't hurt the system. But at the same time, we want it to be something for which the results of our edit will be noticed. Right-click on the Start button and click Explore. This will open Windows Explorer.

2. Click View>Folder Options. Now click on the View tab. This will bring up the window seen in **Figure L14-4**. Note the line that reads "Remember each folder's view settings." You're about to change that.

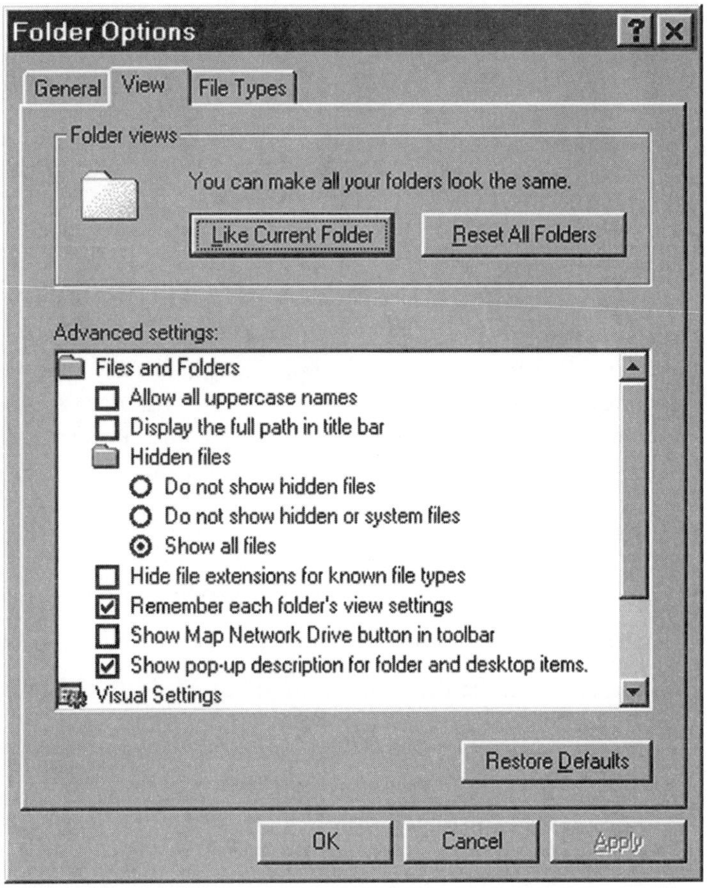

Folder Options

General | View | File Types

Folder views

You can make all your folders look the same.

[Like Current Folder]   [Reset All Folders]

Advanced settings:

- Files and Folders
  - ☐ Allow all uppercase names
  - ☐ Display the full path in title bar
  - 📁 Hidden files
    - ○ Do not show hidden files
    - ○ Do not show hidden or system files
    - ⊙ Show all files
  - ☐ Hide file extensions for known file types
  - ☑ Remember each folder's view settings
  - ☐ Show Map Network Drive button in toolbar
  - ☑ Show pop-up description for folder and desktop items.
- 📁 Visual Settings

[Restore Defaults]

[OK]   [Cancel]   [Apply]

Figure L14-4   Folder viewing options in Windows Explorer

3. In the registry editor, open the HKEY_LOCAL_MACHINE> Software>Microsoft> CurrentVersion>explorer>advanced> folder. Highlight ClassicViewState in the navigation area. On the topic area, several entries will appear. Double-click on Text. In the Edit String field that appears, type in the words These are Equal Opportunity Folders and click OK.

4. Close and restart Windows Explorer. It is not necessary to restart the machine. Now when you view folder options, how does that entry read?

EXERCISE 3: THE SCANREG UTILITY

Of course, now you want to put things back the way they were. Obviously, the easy was it to browse to that Registry entry and type in the words the way they used to be. But what if you can't remember how it used to read? Or if you can't remember what entry you edited. Or worse yet, Windows blue-screens just as it's entering the graphical mode. There must be a way to roll back the system to a previous setting. And in fact, there are two. The first is, of course, to open the Registry editor and click Registry>Import Registry File and then select the backup of the registry that you made. But that's too easy and doesn't give me the chance to show you the ScanReg utility. Windows 2000 and 2003 users unfortunately don't have this utility.

1. Restart your machine and as POST is completing, just before Windows starts to boot, start pressing the F8 key. This will bring up a boot menu. One of the options is to start Windows to a Command Prompt. Select this option and continue booting. This will bring you to a C:\ prompt.

2. Type scanreg at the command prompt. The ScanReg utility will start and the first thing it will do is to scan the registry for errors. You can't stop this process despite the fact that, in all the years I've used this utility, no matter how corrupted the registry was, ScanReg always reported no errors.

3. Next you are prompted to either back up your registry or to view existing backups. Obviously if you're having a problem with the current version of the Windows registry, the last thing you want to do is make a backup of a corrupted registry. Tab over to View Backups. You will see four versions of registry backups listed by the date they were created. Pick the backup previous to the one with today's date and select Restore. After a few moments, it will prompt you to restart your machine. And Windows will boot to the older backup without the changes you made.

Lab Summary

One of the things I hope you learned from this lab is that every aspect of how Windows performs is a function of some entry in the registry. In Lab Seven, you learned how to make safe changes to the registry in Control Panel. This lab demonstrated the basics of how the Registry Editor can be used to make changes beyond the scope of Control Panel. And, at the risk of sounding like a skipping CD, before you mess around with the registry, *back it up!!!*

Lab Review

1. Which Registry key is not stored in a file, but rather is created on the fly as the system boots?

2. List two different ways to back up the full Windows registry?

3. You have just installed a new video card. During the driver installation you asked to see a list of all devices. You are so used to another computer that you use every day that you mistakenly selected a completely different make and model of video card. Now every time you boot your machine, as soon as the Windows graphical interface starts to load, the screen goes blank. How might you fix this? (There are actually a few ways. If you come up with a way I did not discuss in this lab, you should lobby the instructor for extra credit.)

4. Which primary key holds the user settings for every user with an account on the system?

5. How many backups of the Registry does Windows 98 maintain?

15

MANAGING PRINTERS IN WINDOWS

CompTIA Objectives Covered In This Lab
1.3 Know the basic purpose and function of the basic types of server. (File/Print)
3.4 Configure external peripherals.

The process of printing in any operating system is one that baffles many. It just seems to happen. As a technician, however, you need to be able to install and configure printers, and then over the course of time, make sure that printer keeps doing what it has to do. To be certain, a lot of this work is hardware related, but the software side is every bit as critical. Updating and reinstalling drivers, mapping networked printers, and managing the print spool are all part of the job. Those are the things I go over in this lab.

EXERCISE 1: INSTALLING A PRINTER

This is one of those labs where it really doesn't matter what version of Windows you have installed on the system. The procedure doesn't change; only the pictures change. The biggest difference is that with WIN2K or Server 2003, the process of installing a local printer is so automated there is rarely much for the technician to do except supply the disk.

I should point out that installing a network printer is part of the process of managing printers. However, because you will not build your network for a couple of more labs, I've decided to include that as part of the networking lab. So for now, I'll concentrate on installing a local printer.

1. Open the Printers applet from the Control Panel. There are three ways to do this. The first is to double-click on My Computer, and then double-click on the Printers icon. Another way is Start>Settings>Control Panel and double-clicking on the Printers icon. To me, both of these methods are more cumbersome than simply clicking Start>Settings>Printers. In Server 2003, there is a specific shortcut to Printers and Faxes in the Start Menu, so it is even easier. Whichever method you choose as your own, you'll end up with a screen like the one in **Figure L15-1**.

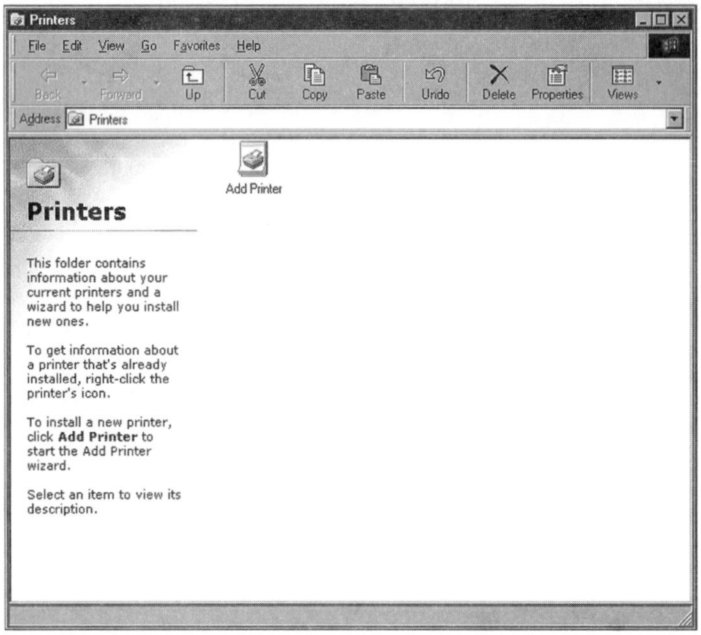

Figure L15-1   The Printers applet in Windows

2. Because these are fresh installations, there is no printer installed, so your only option at this time is to install a new printer. Double-click on the Add Printer icon to start the Wizard (**Figure L15-2**).

3. Because the next few screens are merely variations on the same theme I won't waste space or time with screen shots. Click Next and in the screen that follows, click Local printer.

4. In the next screen that appears (**Figure L15-3**), you will be presented with a long list of manufacturers supported by the OS in the left-hand pane. When you click on any given manufacturer, a list of printer models appears in the right-hand pane. If you are installing a printer that is not listed, you can click on the Have Disk option to install a third-party driver. Because it is unlikely that most labs will be blessed with an individual printer for each Student PC, we'll simply lie to Windows and tell it we have one.

5. So that everybody stays on the same page, scroll down to the HP entry in the manufacturer's list. You can get there faster by pressing the H key on your keyboard. In the printer model list, select HP Color LaserJet 5/5M PS as seen in **Figure L15-3**. Click Next.

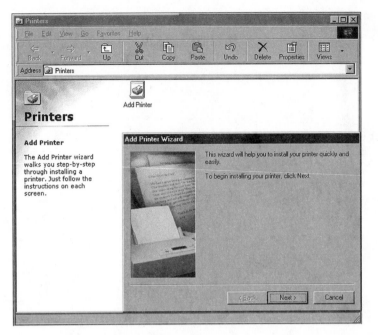

Figure L15-2   Adding a new printer is accomplished by a Wizard.

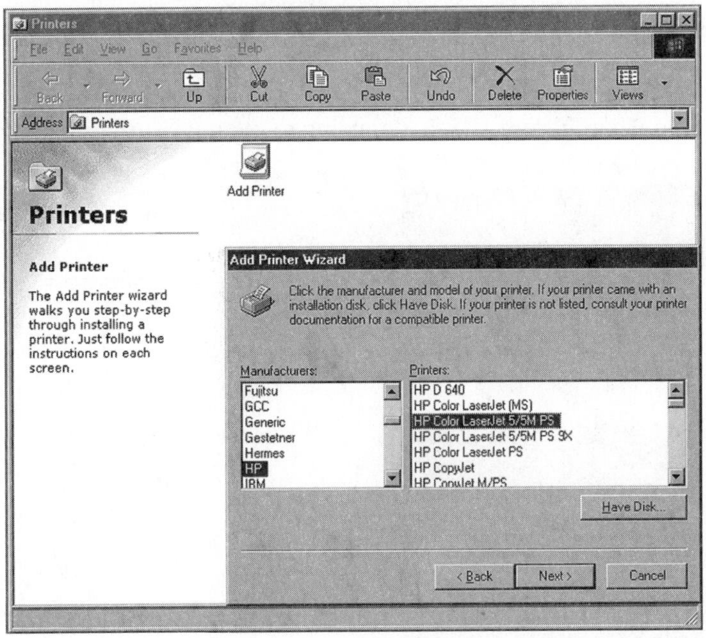

15

Figure L15-3   While 2000 Server supported many printer models, it doesn't come close to the number of printers supported by 2003!

6. Next, the Add Printer Wizard is going ask you what port you want your new printer to print to. In WIN98 the options are somewhat limited. You have the choice of your serial ports, your parallel ports, or to Print to File, as seen in **Figure L15-4**. Printing to file is useful if you have a printer at the office to which you want to output the file. In your case, select LPT1.

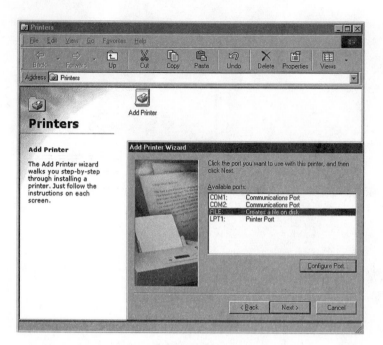

Figure L15-4   WIN98 is somewhat limited in the options available for a destination port. WIN2K and Server 2003 both allow you to print to USB and to configure a TCP/IP port from this window.

7. Now you will be asked to name your printer. A default name will already be filled in. If you like long names, click Next. As you can see in **Figure L15-5**, I'm going to call my virtual printer Color Laser.

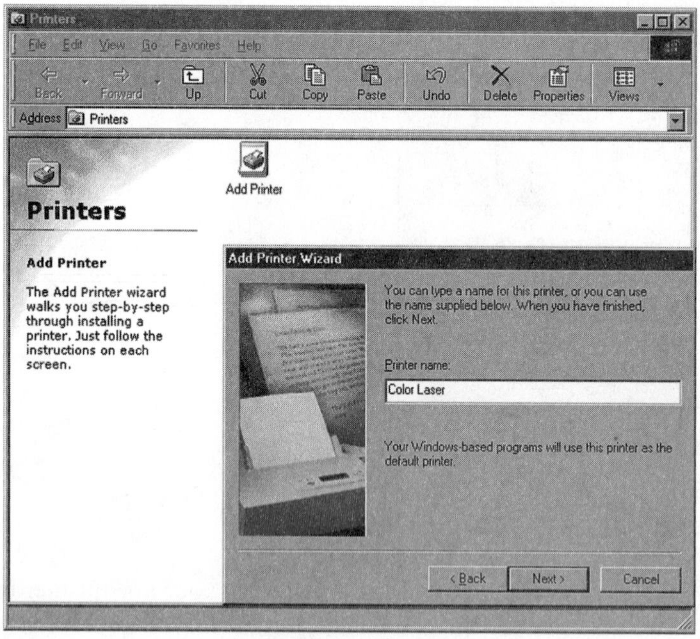

Figure L15-5   You can name your printer whatever you like. Just remember that other people will be seeing it.

8. In the next screen (**Figure L15-6**), you'll be asked if you want to print a test page. Make sure you have the Installation CD in the drive. Under most circumstances, in a new printer installation, you want to click Yes and continue. However, if there is no printer hooked up to your system, click on the No button and click Next. The Wizard will copy several files from the CD.

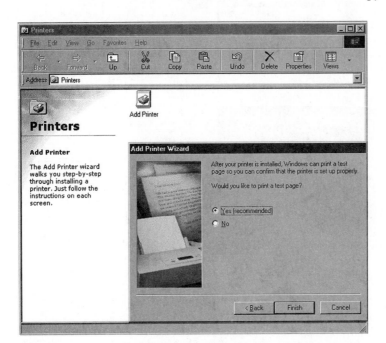

Figure L15-6   Any time you are installing a printer for the first time, it's a good idea to print a test page. That way you know you have connectivity and that you have installed the correct driver.

9. Should you ever choose to print to file, you'll get the screen seen in **Figure L15-7** asking you to name the file. Once the file has been written, you'll get the screen in **Figure L15-8** asking if the page printed successfully. Whenever you have selected a physical port to print to, **Figure L15-8** will be the next screen you see. Click Yes. Congratulations! Your printer is installed.

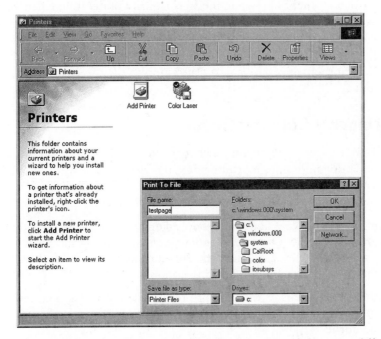

Figure L15-7   Naming a print file when printing to file is no different than in any other application.

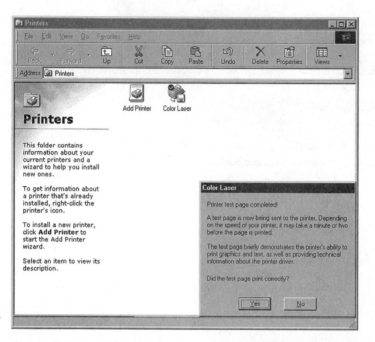

Figure L15-8   When printing to a port, the Wizard will ask you if the test page printed successfully.

Exercise 1 Review

1. You are trying to install a brand-new printer and you realize your make and model isn't on the list of supported printers. What do you do now?

2. What is the extension that allows you to identify a print job that has been printed to file?

EXERCISE 2: MANAGING THE PRINTER QUEUE

One of the handier things about a graphical interface is having a utility that manages something as complex as the printer queue. What is the printer queue? Simply put, the vast majority of the time when a printer is call upon to perform, a single job is sent from the PC to the printer. However, occasionally things go wrong. Perhaps the printer is shared out over a network, or a user prints a barrage of documents in succession. Then suddenly the printer simply says "Enough's enough" and shuts down. The printer queue provides the user or administrator a way to cancel stalled print jobs, or even bring a critical job to the top of the list when there are numerous jobs waiting in the queue. I'll show you how.

Exercise 2a: Removing Documents from the Queue

In the event that a document freezes, or a networked computer locks up while printing a document, the stalled document will prevent all other documents from printing. If you're not familiar with the workings of the printer queue, this can be a perplexing problem. Everything is working properly, except the letter to your mother-in-law won't print. Remove the offending document and all should be well.

1. Create an offending print job. With no physical printer hooked up, that should be easy to do. Click on Start>Programs>Accessories>WordPad. Open C:\Windows\script.doc by clicking File>Open and browsing to the Windows directory. Most likely that's the only document you will find available. It's a document file that should exist on any fresh Windows installation.

2. Press <Alt>+P to print the document. As the only printer installed, your Color LaserJet will be selected as the default printer. Press <Enter>. Repeat this step about four times until you have several documents in the queue.

3. Click on Start>Settings>Printers to open the Printers applet (or Printers and Faxes in Server 2003). Double-click on the installed printer's icon to open the window shown in **Figure L15-9**.

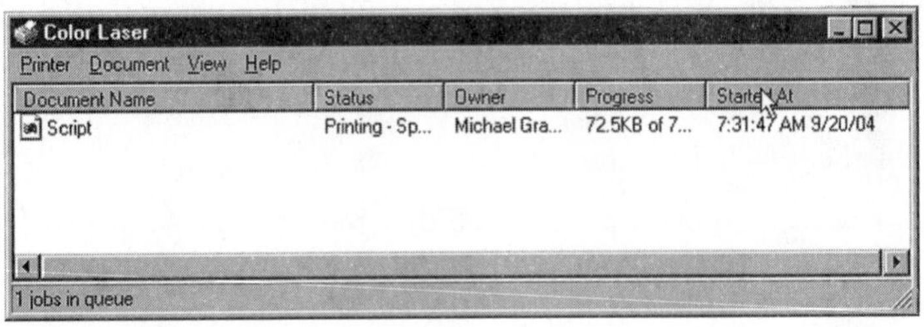

Figure L15-9 The Windows Printer Queue

4. All of your attempts to print will be visible in this screen. In the Window Title Bar, you will see that the printer is listed as Offline. The information you can learn from this small applet includes the status of the print job, the person who originated any particular print job (useful in a networked environment), how far along the current job is, and what time any given job was initiated.

5. To remove a single document from the queue, highlight that document and on the menu, click Document>Cancel, as seen in **Figure L15-10**. That job will be deleted.

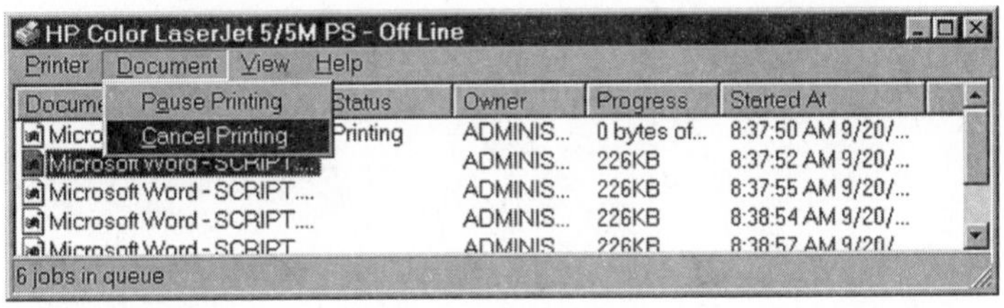

Figure L15-10 Canceling a single document from the queue

6. On rare occasions, the printer queue itself may lock up, or you may have to bring a printer offline for an extended period. In either case, you will most likely find it desirable to flush the printer queue completely. In order to do this, open the queue for the targeted printer, and as seen in **Figure L15-11**, click on Printer>Purge Print Documents. Most frequently the document that is attempting to print will not clear itself using this method, so you would revert to the method discussed in the previous step for deleting a single print job.

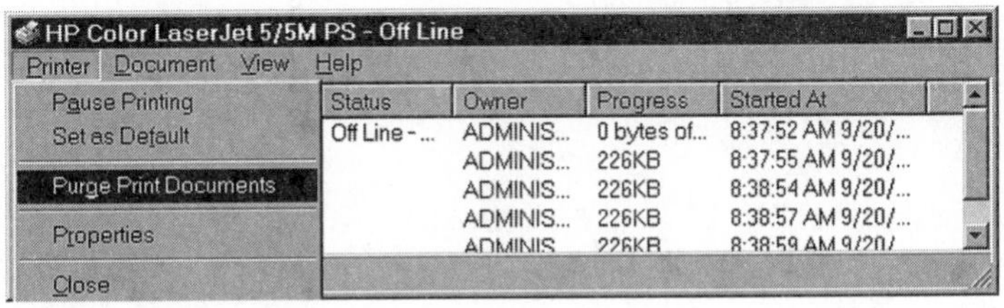

Figure L15-11 Purging the Printer Queue

Exercise 2a Review

1. Describe the process of deleting a single job from the Printer Queue.

2. How would you flush all print jobs from the queue?

Exercise 2b: Moving A Document To A Different Position In The Queue

In a busy office, the only printer can sometimes get quite busy. What if you have an important meeting coming up in ten minutes and you realize you need a critical document printed? You shoot it off to the printer and realize that there are 6 jobs ahead of you and 2 of them are copies of the boss's 800-page novel. Can you scoot your job ahead of those marathon toner-bleeders? Sure you can. Here's how.

1. Open the printer queue for the selected printer.

2. Click on the print job you want to move up, and slide that job up underneath the job that is currently printing. Your job is now next in line. You can also move print jobs down in this same manner if you simply want to move a job to the bottom of the stack.

Exercise 2b Review

1. What is the procedure for moving a print job up or down in the queue?

2. What happens if you keep moving the boss's print jobs to the bottom of the order?

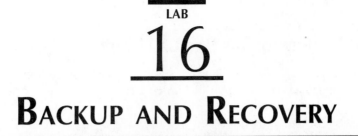

16

BACKUP AND RECOVERY

CompTIA Objectives Covered in this Lab

1.2 Identify basic concepts and procedures for creating, viewing, and managing files, directories, and disks. This includes procedures for changing file attributes and the ramifications of those changes (for example, security issues).

The following exercises will provide a brief overview of the Windows backup utility. Then we will go through the process of performing a backup and subsequently deleting and restoring the data we backed up. Optimally, in order to do this lab, each computer should be equipped with a tape backup unit. However, it is assumed that is not the case in the majority of classrooms and the backup will be done to the file in these exercises.

EXERCISE 1: AN OVERVIEW OF THE BACKUP UTILITY

1. To start W2K backup, click on Start>Programs>Accessories>System Tools>Backup. This will bring up the screen shown in **Figure L16-1**.

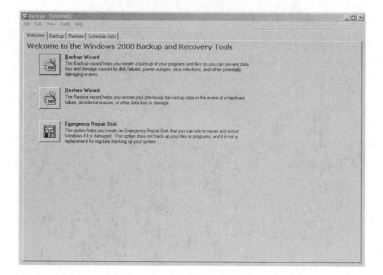

Figure L16-1   The Windows Backup Utility

2. The three options shown in this window are Backup Wizard, Restore Wizard, and Emergency Repair Disk. We won't be working with any of the Wizards in this lab. We'll be learning to manual backup and recovery.

3. Click on the Backup tab. You should now have a window like that in **Figure L16-2**. Note that you can back up any or all of your local drives from your CD-ROM drive, the System State, and from Network Places. If you click on your C: (or any other) Drive, it will show the various folders on that drive. You can selectively choose which files and folders to back up.

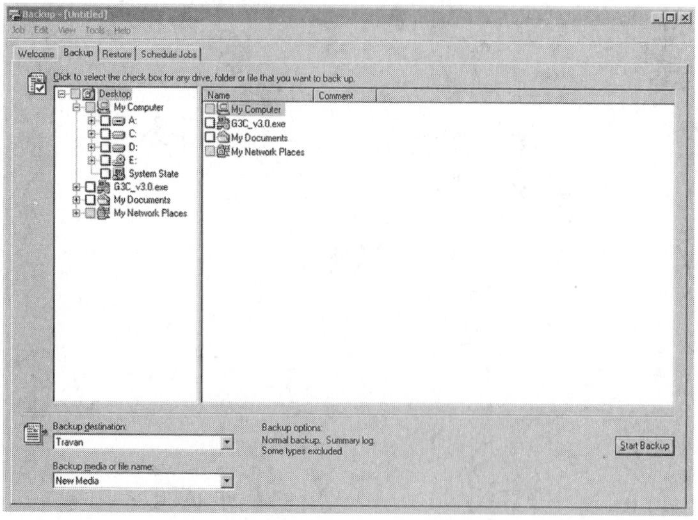

Figure L16-2   Backup options

4. At the bottom of the screen are two other options. Backup destination: allows you to select where that file is going to be stored. If you have no tape drive installed on your machine, the only option will be File. Note in **Figure L16-3** that I have the option to backing up to a miniQIC, Travan, or File. Backup media or file name allows you to indicate the form of medium you are going to use or select a file name (with full director path) for your backup.

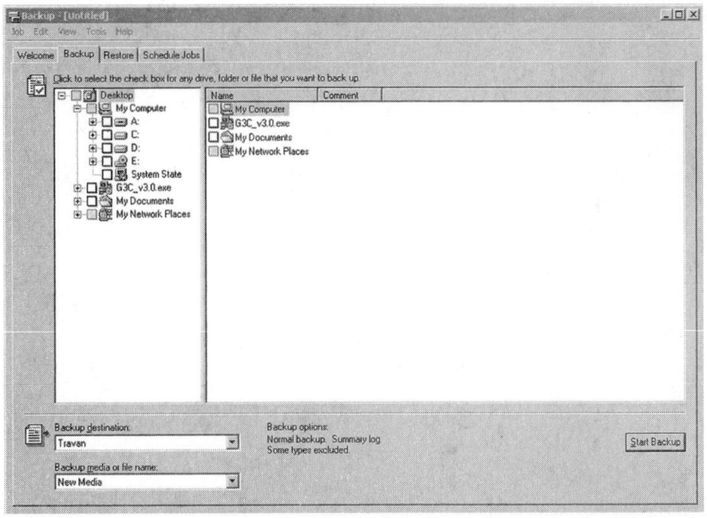

Figure L16-3 Selecting the destination for your backup

5. Now click on the Tools option in the menu and select Options (**Figure L16-4**). Under Backup Type, we can select Normal, Copy, Differential, Incremental, or Daily. We'll be looking at this section in detail in Exercise 2, so for now, let's move on to the next section.

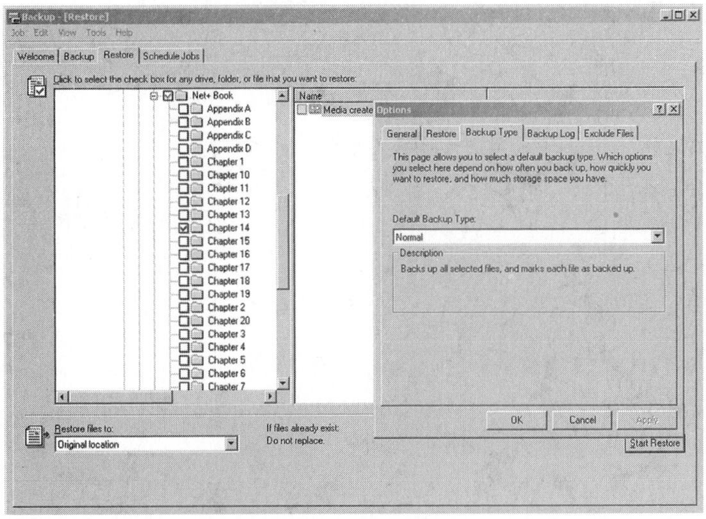

Figure L16-4 Selecting the backup type

6. Click on the Restore tab. In this screen (**Figure L16-5**), you are presented with all possible locations on your computer where a backup could exist. If you have no tape drive installed on your machine, the only option available to you will be File.

7. In **Figure L16-5**, I have opened the Travan option to show that my last backup included my C: drive and my D: drive. In **Figure L16-6**, I have opened the contents of the D: drive. When you do this, your tape drive will go into action as it tries to load the contents of that folder. Once it has done that, it will rewind the tape. This can take several minutes on Travan drives. DAT or DLT drives are usually somewhat quicker.

8. Notice that by clicking on just a single subdirectory or file (as I've done in **Figure L16-6**), I can restore just that file or directory. By clicking on an entire drive, I will restore the contents of that entire drive.

Figure L16-5   Restore options in the Windows Backup Utility

Figure L16-6   The Windows Backup Utility allows you to selectively restore files.

Exercise 1 Review

1. Where do we find the backup utility in Windows Server?

2. What is the difference between a differential backup and an incremental backup?

3. What is the difference between copying your files and backing them up?

EXERCISE 2: PERFORMING A BACKUP

In this exercise, we will back up a single directory on our hard drive to a file. In order to expedite the procedure, we will select a small directory. We will use the one we created using our own first name.

1. On the Backup screen, click on the Backup tab. Highlight the hard disk drive that contains your folder, and then click the checkbox next to that folder (**Figure L16-7**).

2. Under Backup destination, select File, and under Backup media or file name, change A:\backup. bkf to C:\backup.bkf. (Note that in the real world, backing up files from your hard drive to your hard drive is not a very sane practice. If your hard drive fails, it all fails; not just selected directories!)

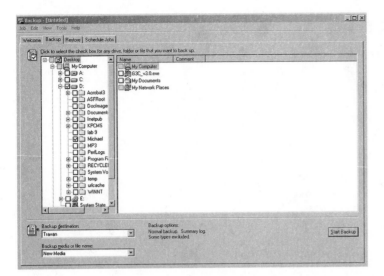

Figure L16-7 Selecting the files to be backed up

NOTE Most backup software still offers the option of backing up your files to floppy. This is a viable option for backing up just a few files or it can be used when you have a file that is too large to fit onto a floppy disk. The Backup utility will split large files onto several floppy diskettes. If you wish, you can back up your entire hard drive to a collection of floppy diskettes. However, I would like to go on record as saying that the idea of backing up my 40GB hard disk to 27,778 diskettes in not a project that is close to my heart.

3. Click <u>S</u>tart Backup. Because we have selected an extremely small backup set, this should only take a second or two. When it is finished, you will get a screen like the one in **Figure L16-8**.

16

Figure L16-8 The Backup Progress Screen

4. Here you are informed of the time and date of the backup along with whether it was successful or not. In addition, you can see how long the backup took, how many files were processed, and the total number of bytes that were backed up. Now click on the <u>R</u>eport button.

5. For **Figure L16-9**, I performed a backup to my tape drive of the My Documents folder on my hard drive. In order to generate some failure messages, I left a few Microsoft Word documents open. Notice the number of files that were skipped because they were in use. This is a key reason network backups should be performed when the fewest users (none at all, if possible) will be active on the network.

```
backup01.log - Notepad                                                    _ □ ×
File  Edit  Format  Help
Backup Status
Operation: Backup
Active backup destination: Travan
Media name: "Media created 10/23/2002 at 1:00 PM"

Backup of "C: "
Backup set #1 on media #1
Backup description: "Set created 10/23/2002 at 1:00 PM"
Backup Type: Normal

Backup started on 10/23/2002 at 1:04 PM.
Backup completed on 10/23/2002 at 1:32 PM.
Directories: 4
Files: 180
Bytes: 826,099,901
Time:  28 minutes and  3 seconds
Media name: "Media created 10/23/2002 at 1:00 PM"

Backup of "D: "
Backup set #2 on media #1
Backup description: "Set created 10/23/2002 at 1:00 PM"
Backup Type: Normal

Backup started on 10/23/2002 at 1:32 PM.
Warning: The file \Documents and Settings\Administrator\Application
Data\Microsoft\Outlook\outcmd.dat in use - skipped.
Warning: The file \Documents and Settings\Administrator\Application
Data\Microsoft\Templates\Normal.dot in use - skipped.
Warning: The file \Documents and Settings\Administrator\Application
Data\Microsoft\Word\AutoRecovery save of Assault on Christian Island, ver 3.asd in
use - skipped.
Warning: The file \Documents and Settings\Administrator\Application
Data\Microsoft\Word\STARTUP\PDFMaker.dot in use - skipped.
Warning: The file \Documents and Settings\Administrator\Local Settings\Application
Data\Microsoft\Outlook\outlook.pst in use - skipped.
```

Figure L16-9   Viewing the backup log

Exercise 2 Review

1. What types of destination locations are supported by Windows Server?

2. Why would we not want to back up our hard drive to floppy diskettes?

3. How can we find out if all of our files were backed up when the operation is completed?

4. If not all files were backed up, what are some possible causes?

EXERCISE 3: PERFORMING A RESTORE OPERATION

Restoring data to a hard disk drive need not be cause for panic. From your restore file, you have the option of performing a complete restore (as would be required after a hard disk failure once the disk was replaced) or restoring selected files (as might be necessary if a single file is inadvertently deleted, overwritten, or corrupted.) In this exercise, we will delete our folder that we just backed up and use our backup file to recover our lost data.

1. First, go into Windows Explorer and delete your folder. Because you shared this folder out in an earlier lab, you will be warned that other people might be using the folder. Click OK.

2. In the Backup utility, click on the Restore tab. Click on the + next to File and highlight the media set you created in Exercise 2 (**Figure L16-10**).

3. Check the box next to your folder. Make sure that the option Restore files to: has Original location selected and click the Start Restore button. The Confirm Restore screen will appear (**Figure L16-11**) and offers the choice of starting your Restore or selecting Advanced Options.

4. Click on the Advanced button. We don't really need to use any of these options, but now is a good time to explore them, because we are here anyway. These options include:

   a. Restore security: This should be checked by default. It makes sure that all permissions assigned to this folder and the files it contains remain intact.

   b. Restore Removable Storage database: Removable Storage is a Windows service that allows applications to access and share resources stored on removable media. Unless you have installed and configured Removable Storage on your system, it is not necessary to select this option.

   c. Restore junction points, and restore file and folder data under junction points to the original location. A junction point is a physical location on your hard drive that points to another physical location or another storage device. It's a good idea to always leave this box checked. There may be no junction points required, but it's better to have it and not need it than to need it and not have it.

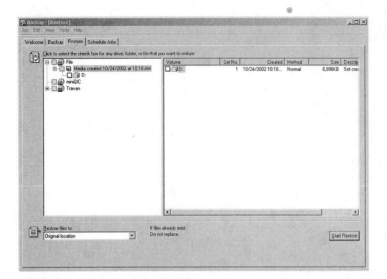

Figure L16-10   Selecting the files to be restored

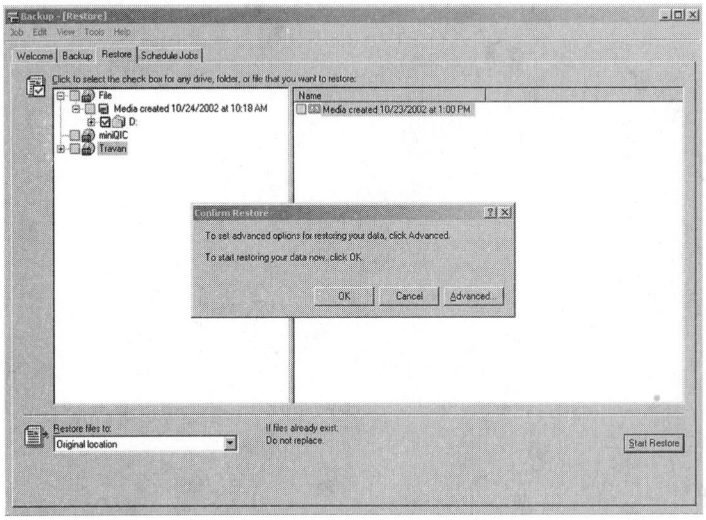

Figure L16-11   The Confirm Restore screen

16

      d. When restoring replicated data sets, mark the restored data as the primary data for all replicas. This is most likely grayed out on your screen. It assures that information used by the File Replication service knows whether this data should be replicated to other servers on the network.

      e. Preserve existing volume mount points: This particular option only makes a difference when restoring an entire drive. If you are installing a new drive and it has been partitioned, it is best if this option were not checked. Otherwise, new partitions will be created on the drive.

5. For this exercise, none of these options are needed. So click Cancel to get back to the Confirm Restore screen and click OK. You will be prompted to enter the location of the backup file. C:\backup.bkf should be the default location (**Figure L16-12**). Click OK.

6. You will briefly see a Restore Progress screen flashing the files as they are restored, and then settle into the screen seen in **Figure L16-13**. As you can see, it is identical to the Backup Progress screen we saw in the previous exercise. It, too, offers the option of viewing a report, which will be identical to the one we looked at in that exercise.

7. Go to Windows Explorer again. You should be able to browse to your folder and see that all contents are intact.

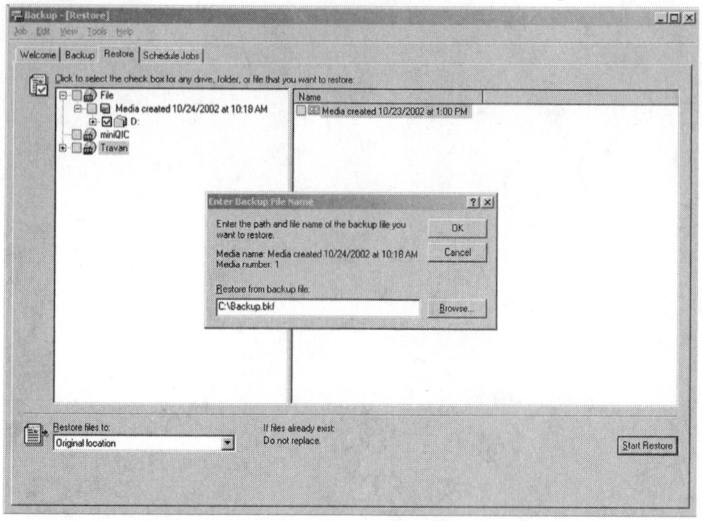

Figure L16-12   Confirming the location of backup files

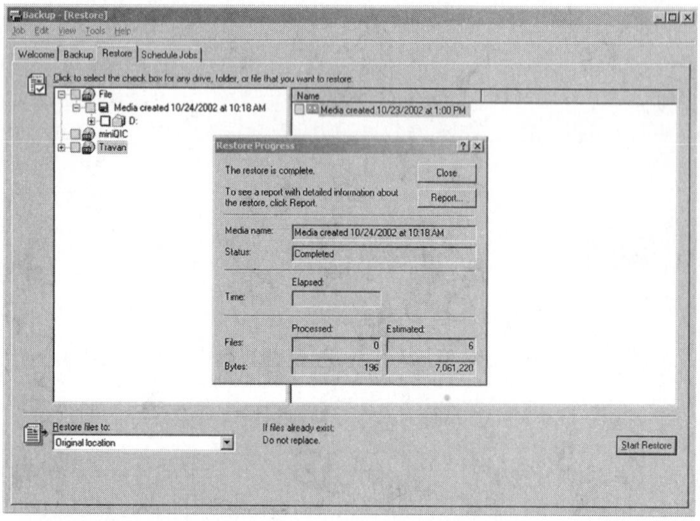

Figure L16-13   The Restore Progress screen

Exercise 3 Review

1. One of our users has inadvertently overwritten a critical file on the server. Can we get just that file back, or do we have to restore the whole system?

2. Name some of the advanced options available.

EXERCISE 4: SCHEDULING UNATTENDED BACKUPS

In this area, the Windows backup utility is a substantial improvement over previous versions of Microsoft's backup utilities. In this exercise, we'll see how to schedule different backups to occur on different days of the week. We'll set up our machines to do a full backup on Friday evening at 8:00 P.M. and then do incremental backups at the same time Monday through Thursday.

1. In the Backup utility, click on the Schedule Jobs tab. This will bring up the screen shown in **Figure L16-14**.

2. Click <u>A</u>dd Job in the lower right-hand corner of the screen. This starts the Backup Wizard (**Figure L16-15**).

3. Click <u>N</u>ext. The following screen offers three options.

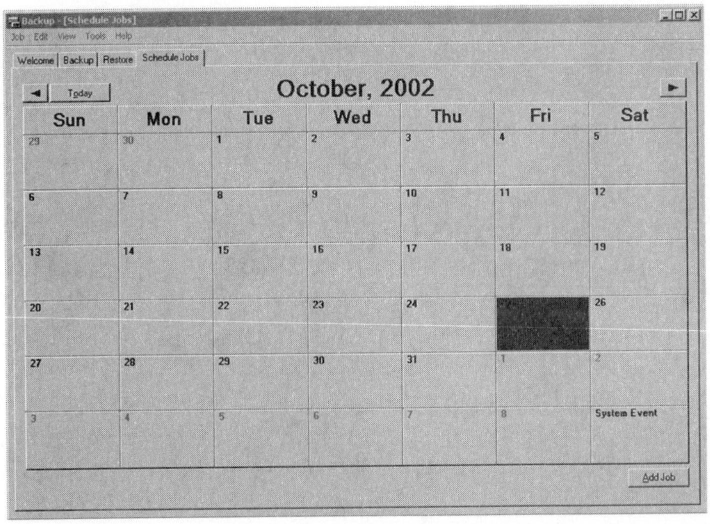

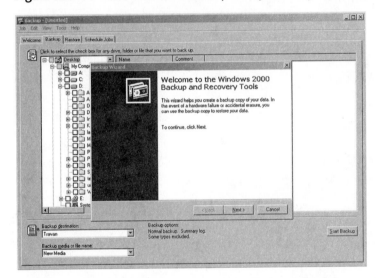

Figure L16-14   The Windows Backup Utility allows you to schedule unattended backups.

Figure L16-15   Adding a new job to the backup schedule

a. Back up everything on my computer: Does just what it suggests. However, don't put too much faith in what it says. As we saw earlier, open or locked files will not be backed up.

b. Back up selected files, drives, or network data: Allows you to choose what material should be backed up.

c. Only back up the System State data: This information includes the files that make up the registry, the COM+ registration database and all system boot files.

4. Select Back up everything on my computer and click Next. This brings up the screen in **Figure L16-16**, where you are prompted to select the destination for your backup. In my illustration, I'll select my Travan drive.

5. In **Figure L16-17**, we are prompted to enter the type of backup we'll be performing. The options are:

a. Normal: Copies all selected files and clears the attribute bit, marking them as backed up. If an entire drive was selected, this is the equivalent of a Full backup.

b. Copy: It copies all selected files but does *not* clear the attribute bit. Therefore, the files will not be marked as backed up.

c. Incremental: Copies any files that were added or changed since the last Normal or Incremental backup. It clears the attribute bit, marking the files as backed up. All subsequent incremental backup will now back up all files changed since the last incremental backup.

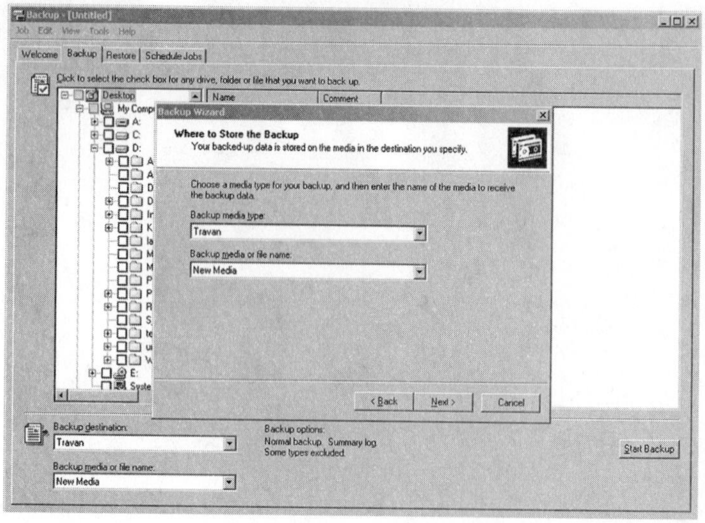

Figure L16-16 Selecting the destination device for your scheduled backups

    d. Differential: This selection copies all files that were added or changed since the last Normal or Incremental backup, but does *not* clear the attribute bit. Therefore, files will not be marked as backed up. All subsequent differential backups will back up all files added or changed since the last Normal or Incremental backup, but not those that changed since the last Differential backup.

    e. Daily: Copies only files that were added or changed on the day the backup is created. The attribute bit is not cleared.

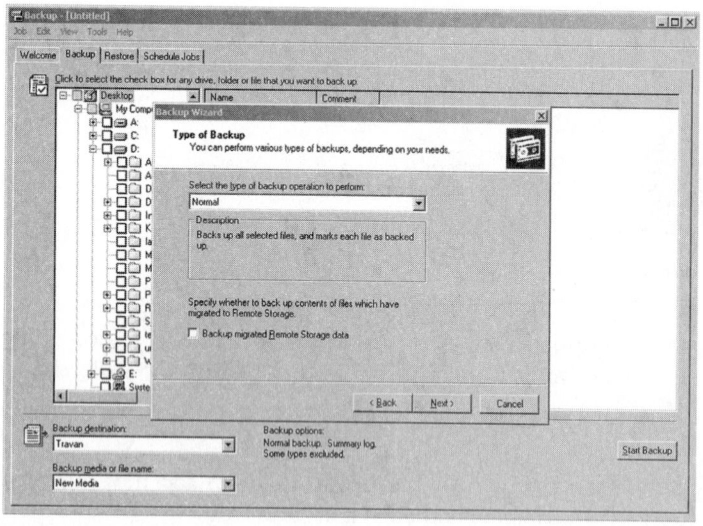

Figure L16-17 Selecting the type of backup to be performed

6. Because we are creating a full backup, select Normal, and click <u>N</u>ext. The Backup Wizard now asks you how you want to back your data up (**Figure L16-18**). Two independent options are offered.

    a. <u>V</u>erify data after backup: This option compares each copy of the file to the original when the backup has been completed. This can add a substantial amount of time to the backup but adds security for your data.

    b. Use <u>h</u>ardware compression, if available: This allows you to pack more data onto a single tape and reduces the amount of time it takes for a backup to be completed.

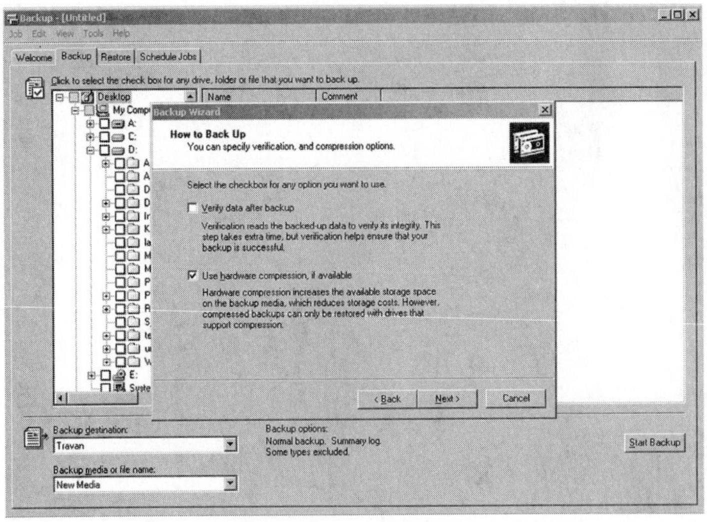

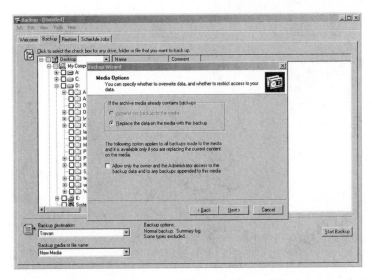

Figure L16-18   Configuring the backup

7. Click Next. You will be given the Media Options screen (**Figure L16-19**). Normally, you would be using the same tapes repeatedly. In this case, you would make sure that the option Replace the data on the media with this backup is selected. If the data is sensitive data, you can add a bit more security by selecting the option Allow only the owner and the Administrator access to the data and to any backup appended to this media. The latter option is not selected by default.

Figure L16-19   You have to tell the backup utility how media is to be handled.

8. The Backup Label screen now appears (**Figure L16-20**). This is the information that you should write onto the label of the tape before storing it. Click Next.

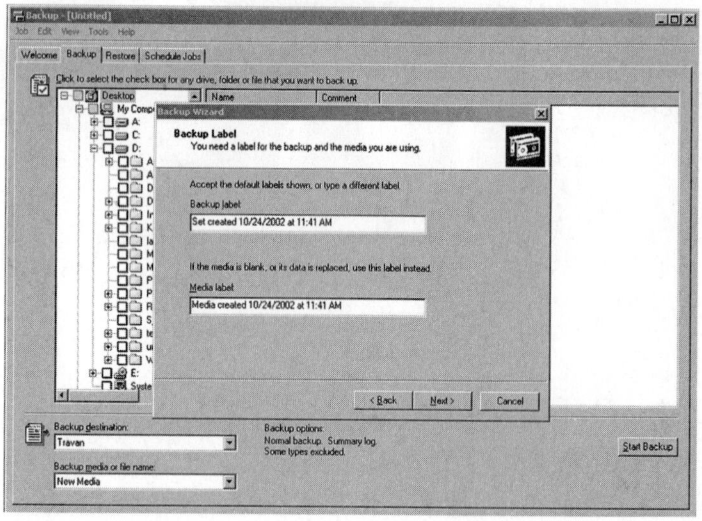

Figure L16-20   The Windows Backup Utility reminds you to label your backup tapes.

9. Now you'll be prompted as to when you want your backup to occur (**Figure L16-21**). Select Later and give your job a name. We'll call it Weekly Full.

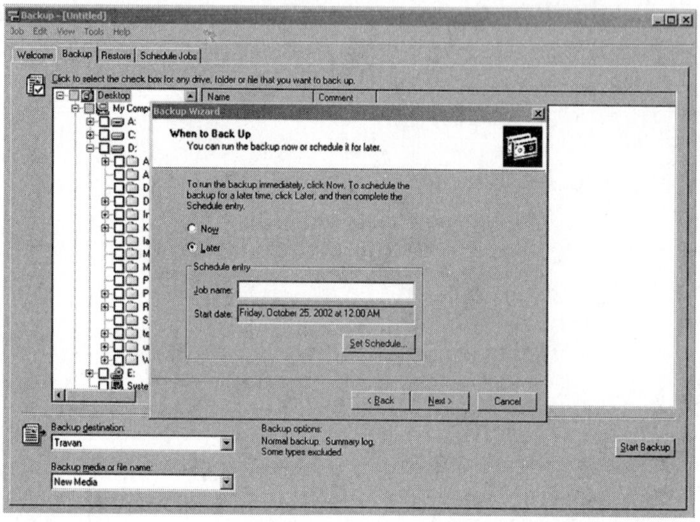

Figure L16-21   You must tell the scheduler what time you want these backups to occur. Choose a time when there will be the fewest users on the network.

10. Now click on the Set Schedule button. Under Schedule Task, select Weekly. Under Start Time, select 12:00 A.M. Under Schedule Task Weekly, select 1 for Every and click the Friday checkbox, as in **Figure L16-22**. Make sure that all other days are deselected.

11. Click OK and on the Backup Wizard screen, click Next. This will bring up the Completing the Backup Wizard screen as seen in **Figure L16-23**. Click Finish and you are done.

12. Now, on the Schedule Jobs calendar, little icons with a blue N (for Normal) will appear on all Fridays from this date forward.

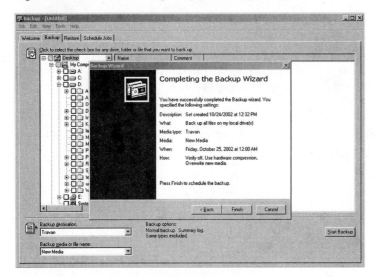

Figure L16-22   Scheduling daily or weekly events

Figure L16-23   Finishing the Backup Wizard

13. To schedule daily differential backups, repeat the above procedure except for two key differences. In step 5, where we configured backup type, select differential. In step 10, where the events are scheduled, select Weekly as before, but check the boxes for Mon, Tue, Wed, and Thu. Under Job name call it Daily Differential. Finish the Wizard, and icons will appear on all Mondays through Thursdays with a green D (for differential). Your calendar should now resemble **Figure L16-24**.

14. This is the most important step of all. Make sure there is a tape in the drive for each day an event is scheduled. It may seem like a no-brainer, but an empty tape drive is undoubtedly the most common cause of backup failure.

> **NOTE** You may notice if you look carefully that there is no option in the Backup Scheduler to delete a scheduled event. If you need to delete a scheduled backup for any reason, open Control Panel and double-click on Scheduled Tasks. Highlight the job you want to delete and press the delete key on your keyboard. It will ask you if you're sure. Click OK and the jobs are gone.

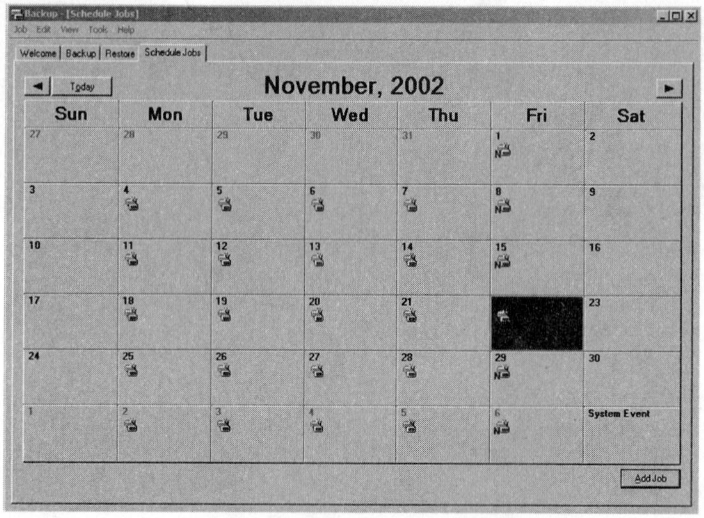

Figure L16-24   A Scheduling Calendar with events in place

Exercise 4 Review

1. We want to schedule our server to perform a Full backup every week, starting at 12:00 a.m. on Saturday. However, we want our daily backups to be differential backups and to run at 10:00 p.m. every other night. How do we keep these from conflicting?

2. What is the primary cause of backup failure in unattended scheduled backups?

3. We need to delete one or more scheduled backup jobs. But there is no delete function in the backup utility. How do we do that?

APPENDIX

A

ANSWERS TO REVIEW EXERCISES

Lab 2

Exercise 1

1. Why are you unable to run Tuff Test from your Technicians Boot Diskette?

   Hardware diagnostics must be run independently of the OS in order to eliminate driver issues from the equation.

3. As noted in the lab, in order to test either a serial port or a parallel port using Tuff Test (or most other diagnostics programs, for that matter) a loopback adapter must be installed. Why do you think this is the case?

   These ports need a completed circuit to bring transmitted data back into the machine. You do not want to have an actual device hooked up to the port because that would make it difficult to determine if the port or the device was causing the problems. A loopback adapter returns the signal in a null fashion.

Exercise 2

1. Why do you suppose knowing the make and version of the BIOS of the machine you are testing is so critical?

   It is because not all versions of BIOS check system functions are in precisely the same order.

Lab 3

Exercise 1

1. Using what you learned from the above exercises and from your textbook, explain why changing a few settings in the Advanced BIOS Settings are unlikely to harm your computer, whereas changes in Advanced Chipset settings may prevent your system from booting.

   Advanced BIOS settings control such functions as boot order and whether or not a particular device is enabled or disabled. Advanced Chipset functions alter the way the system interacts with hardware such as memory and the CPU. If you tell your 100 MHz CPU to run at 400 MHZ (assuming your Setup program will let you), it will do just that. For a very short while, anyway.

3. When trying to fine-tune a system, why do you think that seasoned technicians always follow the rule of thumb that states, "Make only one change at a time"?

   Go ahead. Make about 60 changes and then have your system refuse to boot. Now come back and tell me which one of those changes is giving your system heartburn!

5. A user in your company has left the company without notice and password encoded the system they were using before their untimely departure? How are you going to get back into that system?

   If there is a jumper for clearing the CMOS of the motherboard, simply make use of that. If there is not, remove the battery for the proverbial count of 100. Part of resetting to factory defaults is not having a password.

Exercise 2

1. What is the purpose of backing up the CMOS after achieving the optimum configuration?

   If you ever flash your BIOS to a more recent version or if you are forced to reset to factory defaults because of a later change or unknown password, it is easier to make multiple changes this way. And it is harder to forget the one critical change that took you days to figure out.

3. Why doesn't the mouse work while running the CMOSBAK utility?

You are running in a driver-free, command-prompt environment. There are no mouse drivers present to make the mouse functional.

LAB 4

Exercise 1

1. What are the two files you need in order to perform a flash upgrade?

You need the executable flash utility to run the upgrade, and you also need the new BIOS data file to copy to the BIOS chip. Both of these need to be copied to your boot diskette.

Exercise 2

1. What are the three ways of upgrading a flash BIOS that are used by different manufacturers?

Booting from a floppy, flashing from CMOS setup, and flashing from Windows

3. Why does losing power to your machine during the flash have such a disastrous effect?

Flashing a BIOS is an all-or-nothing routine. It first wipes the BIOS chip clean and then copies the new data files to the chip. If power fails after the chip is wiped but before the new code is copied, there is no code on the system that tells the computer how to boot.

Exercise 3

1. What is the number that identifies the manufacturer and BIOS version called?

This is the BIOS Identification String.

LAB 5

Exercise 1

1. You have just opened the enclosure and there are no apparent internal drive bays for a hard disk. Where else might the manufacturer have hidden the drive?

On a server case, drive bays are frequently located as external bays accessed from the front of the computer. On a smaller blade server, they might be adjacent to the power supply.

3. What is the name of the cable commonly used to provide power to the hard drive?

Molex

5. What are the three possible jumper settings for an IDE drive?

Master, slave, and cable-select

LAB 6

Lab Review

1. What different settings might have to be manually configured on an older host adapter?

As with any standard expansion card, you might need to configure an IRQ and an I/O address. In addition, a SCSI adapter needs to have its ID number set as well.

3. You have just installed a new SCSI chain and nothing works. During POST and in Windows Device Manager, the host adapter is recognized. What is a likely reason for failure?

The most likely cause is that you failed to terminate the chain on both ends. Because most SCSI host adapters self-terminate, look to the last device on the chain and make sure it is terminated.

5. How would you configure three different hard drives to work as a single array?

The drives must support logical unit numbers. In this case, you *want* all thee drives to share the same device ID. But to keep the second and third drives from being ignored, you set them to different LUNs. Now all three are recognized as a single device.

Lab 7

Exercise 1a

1. Where in WIN98 is the Startup Disk creation utility located?

In Control Panel>Add Remove Programs

Exercise 1b

1. How many diskettes are needed for the WIN2K installation set?

Four

Exercise 2

1. What were the two choices of file system offered during the Disk Preparation sequence?

FAT or NTFS. It does not let you choose which version of FAT. It does this based on the size of the partition you select.

Lab 8

Exercise 1

1. What are two good counters to watch in order to keep track of memory usage?

Page Faults/Sec and *Available Mbytes* are essential ones. You also might want to add *Pages/Sec* and *Committed Bytes*.

Lab 9

Exercise 1

1. What are two things you need to check before ordering new memory for your system?

There are actually more than two things you should check, but the two absolutely ESSENTIAL ones are (1) determine exactly what kind of memory the server uses and (2) verify that the capacity of the memory modules you wish to purchase are supported by your chipset and BIOS.

Exercise 2

1. What are two differences between installing SIMMs and DIMMs?

A DIMM has two notches along the base whereas a SIMM only has one. A difference that is not visible to the naked eye is that on the DIMM, the conductors on either side of the base are performing totally different functions. On the SIMM, the traces on one side are identical to their counterparts on the opposite side.

Exercise 3

1. List two places to check to determine if the system hardware has recognized your upgrade.

During POST, the amount of memory installed is displayed on the screen. Also, operating systems all have some sort of hardware management utility that will report total memory.

3. How do you check total memory in Linux?

On the Gnome Start button, click Programs>System>System Info. The information you are looking for is in the Detailed Information box.

Exercise 4

1. What is the Windows default setting for computer type on any system?

To adjust memory usage for best use by Programs

3. What is the point of running Defrag before reconfiguring a paging file?

This gives the system the largest amount of contiguous hard disk space that can be made available.

LAB 10

Exercise 1

1. Where do you go to create a new user account in WINXP?

Control Panel>Administrative Tools>Active Directory Users and Computers

Exercise 2

1. What is the difference between a local group and a global group?

There are actually a couple of differences. The most obvious one is that the local group is configured and exists on the local server, whereas the global group is a network-wide account. Another difference is that global groups can become members of local groups, but not vice versa.

Exercise 3

1. Why would you want to copy an account as opposed to simply creating one from scratch?

Because all of the fine-tuning you did to that account, such as the various permissions and privileges, become part of the new account without you taking the time to go through and re-create them all.

Exercise 4

1. What is the disadvantage of deleting the account of a user when they leave the company?

If you delete the account rather than simply disabling it, you will never be able to go back and research items related to the account, such as file ownership and account usage.

LAB 11

Exercise 1

1. What are the two things you need to configure in DHCP to make your server into a DHCP server?

   You need to configure at least one new scope (and its associated exclusions) and then you will need to configure the DHCP options.

3. What is the last thing you must do before your DHCP server is really a DHCP server?

   You need to authorize the server.

Exercise 2

1. What is the process for configuring the options in DHCP?

   Click Action>Configure Options and then select from the list that is provided.

LAB 12

Exercise 1

1. Where did you have to go to install the Subcomponents of Networking Services?

   Control Panel>Add/Remove Programs>Windows Components

Exercise 2

1. What is the role of the forward lookup zone?

   The DNS forward lookup zone is used to resolve computer host names to an IP address.

LAB 13

Exercise 1

1. Where would we find the Event View in Windows 2000?

   Control Panel>Administrative Tools>Event Viewer

3. You have configured your server to audit failed logon attempts. Where are reports of these events logged?

   These would show up in the Security Log.

Exercise 2

1. What kinds of information can we learn from an event if we double-click on it?

   You might learn what memory address was active when the error occurred. If this address coincides with the memory address of a device driver, that can tell you what device was active when the failure occurred. If the error is caused by a service that failed to start, you can find out if that service has any dependencies that might need to be looked at. In many cases, an error is accompanied by hyperlinks to Microsoft's Web page to information specific to the error.

Lab 14

Exercise 1

1. What are the two primary files that contain the Registry?

   SYSTEM.DAT and USER.DAT

3. List the six primary keys of the Registry.

   HKEY_CLASSES_ROOT,   HKEY_CURRENT_USER,   HKEY_LOCAL_MACHINE, HKEY_USERS, HKEY_CURRENT_CONFIG, HKEY_DYN_DATA

5. Where would you look for the settings that dictate how a particular file behaves if double-clicked?

   HKEY_CLASSES_ROOT

Lab Review

1. Which Registry key is not stored in a file, but rather is created on the fly as the system boots?

   HKEY_DYN_DATA

3. You have just installed a new video card. During the driver installation you asked to see a list of all devices. You are so used to another computer that you use every day that you mistakenly selected a completely different make and model of video card. Now every time you boot your machine, as soon as the Windows graphical interface starts to load, the screen goes blank. How might you fix this? (There are actually a few ways. If you come up with a way I did not discuss in this lab, you should lobby the instructor for extra credit.)

   The most common approach is to start Windows in Safe Mode. Do this by holding F5 while the machine boots, or by holding F8 and selecting Safe Mode from the boot menu. Once the machine boots, you can open Control Panel, uninstall the incorrect drivers and install the correct ones. The second method is to press F8 while booting and select Last Known Good. This boots the machine using the registry settings that were in place the last time the machine booted correctly.

5. How many backups of the Registry does Windows 98 maintain?

   Three

Lab 15

Exercise 1

1. You are trying to install a brand-new printer and you realize your make and model is not on the list of supported printers. What do you do now?

   You have two options. You can let Windows search the Internet for drivers (I heard a rumor that it actually worked for somebody once), or you can select "Have Disk" and provide the driver disk for your printer. If you do not have the disk, you can do your own Internet search, download the drivers to a specific location, and then browse to the driver.

Exercise 2a

1. Describe the process of deleting a single job from the Printer Queue.

   Open the printer in Printers and Faxes. Click Document>Cancel.

Exercise 2b

1. What is the procedure for moving a print job up or down in the queue?

   In the Printers applet, select the document you wish to move up or down and simply drag it where you want it in the stack of waiting documents.

Lab 16

Exercise 1

1. Where do we find the backup utility in Windows Server?

   Click Start>Programs>Accessories>System Tools>Backup.

3. What is the difference between copying your files and backing them up?

   When you copy a file, nothing happens to the archive bit in the file tables. A backup resets the archive bit to 0.

Exercise 2

1. What types of destination locations are supported by Windows Server?

   Backup to file, to floppy diskette (my personal favorite), and/or to a tape drive.

3. How can we find out if all of our files were backed up when the operation is completed?

   Check the log by clicking the Report button.

Exercise 3

1. One of our users has inadvertently overwritten a critical file on the server. Can we get just that file back, or do we have to restore the whole system?

   You can retrieve individual files from a backup set. However, the process is very tedious and time-consuming. Therefore, you do not want to let users get in the habit of making that request.

Exercise 4

1. We want to schedule our server to perform a Full backup every week, starting at 12:00 a.m. on Saturday. However, we want our daily backups to be differential backups and to run at 10:00 p.m. every other night? How do we keep these from conflicting?

   All you have to do is create separate jobs for each category of backup. They will not conflict.

3. We need to delete one or more scheduled backup jobs. But there is no delete function in the backup utility. How do we do that?

   Go to Control Panel>Scheduled Tasks and delete the task.